The ORVIS Guide to

TACKLE CARE AND REPAIR

Solid Advice for In-Field or At-Home Maintenance

Ted Leeson

The Lyons Press
Guilford, Connecticut
An imprint of The Globe Pequot Press

Printed in China

10 9 8 7 6 5 4 3 2 1

Design by Maggie Peterson

The Library of Congress Cataloging-in-Publication Data

Leeson, Ted.
  The Orvis guide to tackle care and repair : solid advice for in-field or at-home maintenance / Ted Leeson.
      p. cm. (The Orvis guide series)
    ISBN 1-59228-757-3
  1. Fishing tackle--Maintenance and repair. I. Title. II. Series.
SH447.L44 2006
688.7'91 dc22

ACKNOWLEDGMENTS

MY FIRST THANKS TO TOM ROSENBAUER AND JAY CASSELL, who invited me to take on this project and offered invaluable advice and assistance during its completion.

I'm deeply indebted to a number of experts in the fields of tackle design, manufacturing, and repair who spent more hours than they'd probably care to count patiently explaining, answering questions, and sharing the kind of knowledge that comes only from long experience in both the sport of fly fishing and the fly-fishing business. I am particularly grateful to Norman Bowen, Jim Logan, Bob Murphy, Bruce Richards, Dave Swanson, Jim West, and Ron White. This book would have been literally impossible without their generous, and tireless, efforts.

I'd like to thank Al Buhr for showing me his innovative line-splicing technique and kindly permitting me to reproduce the method in print for the first time.

Finally, I owe a special debt of gratitude to my friend and long-time associate in many fly-fishing projects, Jim Schollmeyer, whose skill behind the camera is evident throughout this book. Thanks.

TABLE OF CONTENTS

INTRODUCTION

GOOD FLY TACKLE IS A PLEASURE TO OWN AND A JOY TO FISH. It becomes, in a way, an investment in the many satisfactions we find in our time on the water. And like all investments, it should be protected so that it continues to return those rewards. Some equipment, such as rods and reels, can well last a lifetime if looked after properly. Other types—lines and wading gear, for instance—are manufactured from less durable materials, tend to see harder service, and so eventually wear out. In either case, however, you can get the most out of your tackle—maximizing both its performance and useful life—if you attend to simple routine maintenance and, in the event of an equipment problem, know how to address the kind of repairs that get your equipment up and running and keep you on the water.

Apart from vintage or collection-grade tackle, which is not covered in this book, there's no reason at all to coddle your gear; it is made to be used, a means to an end rather than an end in itself—and a rather simple means at that. On the whole, fly tackle is relatively uncomplicated. It requires no elaborate assembly, relies on no delicate mechanisms, and, except for reels, which are in fact mechanically pretty straightforward, has virtually no moving parts. And perhaps it is this very simplicity that lures some anglers into believing that their gear requires no upkeep at all, which is only true if you wish to risk equipment failure at a crucial moment, costly repairs, or premature replacement. Instead, the virtue of simple gear is that the upkeep is itself rather simple, and devoting a few moments to your equipment from time to time during the season can help ensure that it stays in top shape and trouble-free.

This book contains advice from experts—the people who design, build, maintain, and repair fly tackle—about how to care for your gear and take on the repair jobs that allow you to keep it all in good working condition. Each chapter covers a piece of equipment from three different perspectives:

- Prevention—measures to prevent damaging equipment in the first place or shortening its usable life.
- Care and Maintenance—routine tasks that prolong the life of your gear and maximize its performance.
- Repair—step-by-step procedures to mend the most common types of equipment breakdown or wear.

And for most types of gear, a fourth category is included:

- Field Fixes—emergency first-aid for tackle problems in the field or on longer trips.

None of the care and repair measures detailed in this book requires expert skills or specialized tools, and none is particularly difficult. All of them are practical, at-home procedures that lie well within the capabilities of an average angler. Some preventive and maintenance tasks should be performed regularly, and it's a good idea to develop the habit and make them second nature—as much a part of your fishing as stringing up a rod. Others require only periodic attention or can be saved for an off-season project.

The immediate payoffs are more reliable equipment, better performance, fewer expenditures on gear, and tackle that's ready to fish when you are. But you may also reap benefits that you didn't anticipate. A great many anglers have discovered that caring for and maintaining gear gives a sense of pride and satisfaction. Whether it's getting one more year out of a favorite pair of waders or keeping a reel in mint operating condition, attending to tackle is itself a way of enjoying fly fishing and staying connected to it even during the times you aren't on the water.

CHAPTER ONE

RODS

MOST DAMAGE OR BREAKAGE TO FLY RODS can be attributed to a single cause—avoidable accident. While modern fly rods are remarkably strong when used in their intended fashion, for elastic bending, they are significantly more fragile when subjected to crosswise shearing forces that come from being stepped on, slammed in doors, guillotined by electric car windows, or crushed by heavy gear thrown atop them. Even rods that break during fishing have often been weakened previously by a sharp blow that has fractured fibers in the shaft material but left little visible record of the event. So it's certainly worth taking some precautions to avoid a mishap.

The information concerning prevention, care, and repair procedures presented in the first part of this chapter pertains primarily to graphite and fiberglass rods. Some of these same ideas, of course, are relevant to split-cane fly rods as well. But because of their materials and construction, cane rods have some special requirements, and these are presented separately in the final section of this chapter, "Bamboo Rods."

PREVENTION

- Transport your rod in a case or a rod rack. Obvious as it sounds, this is one of the simplest ways to protect it. Although transporting a rod by letting it extend through the open back window of an SUV or the sliding window in a pickup truck cab is convenient, it is risky. The shaft is exposed to any number of potential accidents, and on a rough drive, the rod can chatter against a hard surface, which may produce a weak spot.

  A roof-rack carrier or a magnetic hood rack is much better for those short trips between fishing spots. At the very least, break the rod down into shorter sections and lay them flat, where they are less susceptible to damage. When traveling in a boat under power, rack your rod; if there's not adequate storage, hang on to it rather than resting it on a gunnel or transom.

- Protect your rods from heat, especially direct sunlight. Don't leave a rod—cased or uncased—in the sunny back window or cargo area of a vehicle. The rod shaft itself is composed partly of a resin. If the rod is in a flexed position—say, the tip is bent slightly to fit the rod in your car—the combination of excessive heat and tension on the rod can actually cause the resin to become slightly malleable; when it cools down, your rod is essentially molded into the flexed position and permanently warped.

  Ultraviolet rays pose no particular threat to the shaft. Some modern rods are nonetheless treated with a UV-resistant finish—but UV rays can degrade or yellow some types of finishes that are applied over the thread wraps securing the guides.

- When you're gearing up to fish, rig your rod last, after your waders and vest are on, and the car doors and windows are shut and locked; many rods are broken before the first cast is ever made.

- When uncasing the rod to set it up, don't set either ferrule end on the ground where it can pick up particles of dirt. Grit that is trapped in the ferrules when you join the rod acts like sandpaper; it can scratch, score, or abrade the ferrule, and over time cause it to weaken or fit loosely. Dirt wedged into a joined ferrule can also make it difficult to disassemble the rod sections.

- Assemble and take down your rod properly. To set up a rod, join two sections together with a light fit so that the guides are about 15 degrees out of alignment. Hold the two sections as close as possible to the ferrule ends, and push the sections together, at the same time rotating the rod shaft so that the guides come into alignment just as the sections are firmly seated. The fit should be secure, but not overly tight. Too little pressure can cause the sections to come apart when you're fishing or, worse yet, loosen without coming apart. A loose fit can allow some play in the male end of the ferrule, which can lever against the edge of the female ferrule and weaken or crack it.

  When assembling rods of more than three pieces, don't start at the butt and work to the tip. Rather, work from both ends; assemble two or more pieces of the butt section, then two or more of the tip section. Finally, join the upper and lower halves. There's always less risk of an accident when working with short sections like this, and it's easier to align the guides.

  To break down a rod, simply reverse the assembly procedure; twist just a bit as you pull the sections directly apart. When twisting the sections, hold them as close as you can to the ferrules, but grasp the shaft only. Don't apply pressure or torque to the guides to get twisting leverage; they can be bent.

And when pulling, draw the sections straight apart, without bending the rod. When rod sections are stuck tightly together, there is a tendency to lay the ferrule high up and close to your chest and use your hands to pull in opposite directions. Many times, this approach actually bends the rod slightly around your chest, and the flex makes it more difficult to separate the sections.

Almost everyone, from time to time, comes in from a day's fishing and discovers that the rod sections are so tightly joined that they can't be taken apart with a simple twist and pull. Here are few approaches to get the job done:

1.   Sometimes, the problem is simple. Your hands are too wet or slippery to get a good purchase on the rod shaft, particularly at its smaller diameters. Try grasping both sections between pads of a high-friction material—patches of chamois or rubber cut from an inner tube; leather or rubber kitchen gloves also work well. The added grip is often enough to separate the sections.

2.   If the sections are still stuck, try this:

Put the rod behind your back, and grasp the sections close to the ferrule. Position your feet about 18 inches apart with your knees almost touching, and press your knuckles tightly into the backs of your knee joints. The ferrule should be centered between your knees.

Press inward with your hands to keep your knuckles in the knee joints; then draw your knees apart, which pulls your hands and separates the ferrule. To be honest, I'm not exactly sure why this works (though it usually does), but I suspect that using your knees like this keeps the rod sections directly aligned and prevents the inadvertent bending of the shaft that often comes when you use a significant force to pull them apart in front of your body.

3.   If the behind-the-knees approach fails, this last one almost always does the trick, though it takes two people.

With a friend or fishing partner, grab the rod sections as shown. Note that each person has one hand on each rod section and that the hands alternate. The hands in the middle are placed close to the ferrule, which is at the center of the picture, and the hands on the outside positioned as close as possible to the hands on the inside. All the hands are holding only the rod shaft; they are not gripping any guides. On the count of three, pull simultaneously, straight outward.

- Be extra careful when taking down a rod in close quarters—between cars in a parking pulloff, on a porch, and especially indoors. One experienced rod-repair person told me that he sees many rods a year that were damaged when they were disassembled inside a house. Under a strong pull, a stuck ferrule suddenly gives way, the sections jerk apart quickly and unexpectedly, and the rod tip crashes into a wall.
- Never lay a rod section or assembled rod flat on the ground. They are devilishly difficult to see. Even if you avoid stepping on it, you can trip over the leader or line, jerking the rod along the ground and possibly damaging it.
- Once rigged up, don't pin the fly, particularly a large fly or a barbed hook, into the cork grip as you walk to the water. Sudden tension on the line—if you catch it in the brush, for instance—can cause the hook to tear out a chunk of cork. Use the hook keeper. Or bring the leader under the reel, around the back, and over the top; then hook the fly into the first snake guide. (This approach has the added benefit of keeping a bit of fly line outside the tip-top of the rod, and you don't have to work the line/leader connection through the tip-top every time you begin casting.)
- When walking with your rod in hand, carry it with the reel pointing forward and the shaft behind you. If you stumble or fall, you won't jam the rod tip into the ground and risk a break.
- When fishing heavy flies—weighted nymphs, patterns with metal barbell-type eyes, beadheads, and coneheads—adjust your casting style to keep the fly well

away from the rod. Angle your rod slightly to one side rather than casting directly overhead in a vertical plane. On the backcast, slow your timing down just a bit, making sure to pause long enough to let the line, leader, and fly straighten out behind you. On the forward cast, open your loop up a little by dropping the rod tip slightly lower than you would when casting a dry fly to allow plenty of clearance between the fly and rod tip. Crashing a hard, heavy fly into the rod shaft, particularly near the tip, can break it immediately or weaken the shaft to the point where it will fracture under the strain of fighting a large fish or double-hauling a long cast. Even a small beadhead pattern, though not particularly heavy, contains a hard, concentrated bit of weight, and if it travels fast enough, the impact against the rod can damage the shaft.

- Learn to fight fish, especially large ones, properly. Keep the rod tip relatively low, maintaining a shallow angle between the line and rod, and work the fish from the butt of the rod and the reel rather than the rod tip. When you're fighting a fish, imagine a straight line running through the butt of the rod outward; imagine a second straight line running backward through the uppermost part of the flexed tip. The intersection of these two imaginary lines should not produce an angle of greater than 90 degrees. Less is better. (A Florida Keys guide once recommended to me, as a rough rule, that when fighting a large fish, the rod tip should never rise above shoulder level.) A rod angle of greater than 90 degrees has two consequences, both bad: It actually decreases the amount of pressure you're applying to the fish, and it stresses the rod tip. When possible, apply side pressure to a fish; you're less apt to overstrain the rod.

  When fighting a fish, resist the temptation to grab the rod shaft above the grip to get more leverage. In essence, you are shortening the length of rod involved in pressuring the fish and putting more stress on the upper, weaker portion of the shaft.

  Finally, never point the rod back over your shoulder so that the tip bends into a tight, narrow U shape—an unconscious habit many anglers have while landing fish. Many rods are broken this way when a fish suddenly thrashes in the water or bolts off on another run. Once a fish is beached, boated, or netted, immediately strip line off the reel to take pressure off the rod.

- Use a rod weight appropriate for the species you are fishing. Landing a silver salmon or striper on a 4-weight may make for some bragging back at the lodge, but it places unnecessary stress on both the fish and your tackle.

- If your fly becomes snagged, don't try to free it by reefing on the rod and jerking it suddenly and forcefully. If the fly is hung up under water, get upstream of the snag. Pull slowly, at a shallow angle, applying pressure from the butt of the rod. If all else fails, point the rod directly at the snag, taking all pressure off the shaft, and pull on the line; you'll either free the fly or lose it, both of which are better than a broken rod.

- Keep the rod away from possible contact with oils or solvents—outboard motor fuel, for instance—which might damage the rod finish, the finish on a wood insert in the reel seat, and rubber butt caps and winding checks.

- Don't store a rod for extended periods with the reel mounted on it. Over time, grit and dried debris can build up behind the screw-locking ring on the reel seat, and you may have problems when you eventually try to take the reel off. And depending on the materials from which the reel foot and seat are made, the metal-to-metal contact can promote corrosion.

- Finally, whether it's the end of the day or the end of the season, never leave a wet or damp rod in a case. Some years ago, I failed to take this precaution with my favorite steelhead rod; six months later when I removed it from the case, the cork grip was furiously sprouting mold, the varnish on the wood insert had turned to a gooey film, and the locking rings on the reel seat had frozen to the threads.

If you have to case up a wet rod when you're leaving the water, take it out again at home. Wipe off any visible moisture with a dry cloth, and let both the rod and rod bag air-dry before returning them to the case. If the rod has been used in salt water, wash the rod bag to remove any residue that might encourage corrosion when the rod is in storage.

CARE AND MAINTENANCE

The maintenance routine for rods is simple and straightforward, consisting primarily of keeping them clean and dry. And in fact the rod shaft itself doesn't, strictly speaking, need much attention in this regard; washing it is largely a cosmetic matter, though it is easier to inspect a clean shaft than a dirty one for nicks, dings, or scratches that could present potential problems, as explained in the "Checkup" section below.

CLEANING

You can wipe down the shaft with a damp rag to remove dirt and dust. If it's extremely dirty, wash it in soap and warm water, and use a plastic, nonscratch scouring pad to remove bits of dried algae and other stubborn materials. On rare occasions, soap and water won't do the trick. I've accidentally smeared rods with wheel-bearing grease, and once I woke up on a camping trip to find the fly rod I'd propped against a tree the night before spattered with sticky sap. A bit of rubbing alcohol and a soft cloth cleaned things up nicely. Avoid stronger solvents, though; they can damage the rod finish.

Cleaning the reel seat goes beyond cosmetics; sand, dirt, and other contaminants in the reel-seat threads can cause scratching or wear. Use soap and warm water to clean the seat whenever you see a buildup of dirt or dried mud trapped in the threads; a soft toothbrush will scrub it out. The reel seat can also be cleaned with a jewelry-cleaning cloth. It will remove the surface dirt and polish the metal, and it does a particularly handsome job restoring luster to nickel-silver seats.

The ferrules should also be cleaned of any dirt or abrasive residue. Assembling and breaking down a dirty ferrule can eventually enlarge the female end to the point that the sections no longer fit securely together. Simply wash and dry the male end. Use a wet cotton swab to wash the female end and a dry swab to remove the excess moisture.

If you like that showroom look, buff the shaft with a spray-on protectant like Armor All or, as a friend of mine does, with furniture polish. You can, if you wish, apply a very light film of gun oil to the metal components of the seat, but avoid getting oil or lubricants that contain solvents on a wood reel-seat insert or on a rubber fighting butt or butt cap. Oils, and particularly solvents that may be mixed with them, can soften the finish on a wood insert and make it tacky, or degrade rubber.

Saltwater rods need somewhat more, and more frequent, attention—not for the shaft but for the other components. Though the materials used to make rod hardware—stainless steel, titanium, anodized aluminum—resist the corrosive effects of salt water, they are not corrosion-proof. To stay on the safe side, don't let a rod used in salt water sit for more than a day or two without washing it, and this holds whether a rod is used daily or just once a season. Counterintuitive as it may seem, many corrosion problems are experienced by anglers who fish salt water only infrequently; they neglect to clean their rods thoroughly in the mistaken belief that corrosion is unlikely because the tackle has seen so little time on the water. But dried salt deposited on a guide or a reel seat over the course of a day can be just as damaging as that deposited over the course of a week.

You can hose off a rod with fresh water after a day's fishing, but a saltwater rod that is used frequently should be given a more thorough cleaning from time to time, as should a rod that is to be put away for the season. And the best way is to break the rod down and take it into the shower with you. Use a soft toothbrush and soapy water to scrub the areas where dried salt water can accumulate and begin corrosion—the pockets underneath the feet of the guides, the joints where stripping guides are welded, the hoods and threads on a reel seat, the metal ferrule on a detachable fighting butt. Spend a few moments on the guides themselves to remove any film of dried salt water. The residue can produce unnecessary friction that hampers line shooting, accelerate wear on a fly line, or corrode the guides.

Again, you can polish the shaft if you like or apply a thin film of oil to the reel seat, taking care not to let the lubricant come into contact with a rubber butt cap or fighting butt.

Washing a dirty cork grip will certainly improve the appearance of your fly rod, but in some cases it's more than a matter of mere aesthetics. Over time, dirt, oil from your hand, algae, fish slime, fly floatant, sunscreen, and other contaminants can build up to the point where the grip acquires a smooth, slick, almost hard glaze. While this film poses no danger to the cork, it can make the grip slippery and cause you to hold the rod more tightly than is comfortable when casting and fishing, particularly when your hands are wet.

A grip can be cleaned in a couple of different ways. You can lightly sand the cork with 220-grit sandpaper, an approach that allows spot-cleaning of heavily soiled portions of the grip. To protect the other rod components from an accidental scratching with the sandpaper, wrap both the shaft ahead of the grip and the reel seat with masking tape. Sand lightly; you're not trying to remove a lot of cork material, only to take off the film of dirt.

You can also clean the grip by washing it with a soft-scrub-type cleanser and a rag or soft brush, particularly if you intend to repair pits or gouges in the cork. A cleanser will work into these irregular areas and freshen the surface for better glue adhesion. Some of these products contain a small amount of bleach, which can help remove stains from the cork. You may want to mask off the reel seat, though if you are careful in washing the grip, this isn't strictly necessary. But make sure to rinse the grip thoroughly. After cleaning a rod—freshwater or salt—wipe it down with a towel, and then let it air-dry completely.

LUBRICATING FERRULES

Rod ferrules should be periodically lubricated—once or twice a season is usually plenty, but if you are on the water frequently you may wish to lubricate them more often. And whenever I give a saltwater rod a thorough cleaning, I treat the ferrules, since the old lubricant is usually washed off.

The best lubricant is a fairly hard wax, not the tackier types of wax used in fly tying, which readily pick up grit. Ordinary paraffin is ideal. Lightly rub the male ferrule, from base to tip, with a piece of wax, applying just a thin film. Lubricating like this prevents wear and eases assembly and disassembly.

STORAGE

The main storage concern, other than preventing accidental breakage, is keeping the rod dry to prevent mildew on the grip and potential deterioration of finishes used on wood reel-seat inserts. Some anglers prefer to store the rod in the rod bag only, and hang the bag on a peg or nail so that air can circulate around it—a practice that makes particular sense if the rod is stored in an area such as a garage, where temperature and humidity can fluctuate and may cause condensation to form inside a rod tube. Rods stored inside a house, however, can be safely kept in the tube provided the cap is off or at least loose to allow some air exchange.

CHECKUP

It's worth taking the time to give your rod a periodic checkup—once a year or so for rods that see light to moderate use; more often for rods that are fished very frequently; as soon as possible if a rod has been subject to severe stress or impact; and prior to taking a longer trip, particularly to a distant destination. Catching a potential problem in the early stages can allow for repairs before the rod is permanently damaged; at the very least, it can prevent you from bringing a rod that is destined for failure or breakage along on an extended trip, where finding a replacement could be difficult.

When checking over a rod, I find it more efficient to keep a running list of any maintenance or repairs needed rather than stopping to address each problem as I find it. And in fact, inspecting two or three rods, keeping a list for each, can help streamline repairs. You can compile a single list of any supplies that are needed, and then set up only once—to wrap thread, for example, or varnish rod windings—as you make repairs on different rods at a single sitting.

A pocket magnifier of 10X or 20X can help you determine if the damage extends beyond the finish into the graphite or fiberglass material beneath. The carbon fibers used in constructing the rod are a very dark gray or black. If you can see black material at the bottom of a scratch or nick, it is probably a candidate for repair. The rod at the top has some deeper chips that should be taken care of; it will be repaired in the sequence shown on pages 17–21. The rod on the bottom, however, has only light, superficial scratches that don't require repair.

Begin with the shaft, preferably a clean one. Take one section of the rod, and examine it under a strong light, rotating it slowly to inspect the entire surface of the shaft. Look for any nicks, chips, dings, or scratches that represent potential failure points in the shaft. Unfortunately, distinguishing between superficial damage to the rod finish, which is primarily cosmetic, and damage that is serious enough to have injured the fibers of the rod shaft itself is not always a clear-cut matter even for experienced rod-repair people. The extreme cases—a light, superficial scratch in the rod finish, or a deep chip well into the shaft—are obvious even to untrained eyes. But there is a gray area of uncertainty between the two, and it is compounded by the fact that a nick or scratch that could be potentially damaging in the more fragile tip section may be a matter of only minor concern in the sturdier butt section.

If the damage looks more than superficial, flag the spot with a piece of masking tape so you can find it again.

While there are no ironclad, foolproof rules in assessing this kind of damage, my own inclination in the matter is to play it relatively safe. Repairs to the butt section have little disadvantage other than a slight compromise in aesthetics and the time taken to make them, and they may well prevent a problem in the future. Tip-section repairs do add some weight and stiffness to the shaft, and so have the potential to influence the rod action, especially under two conditions—if the tip is damaged in more than one spot, or the rod is designed for a very light line weight. But these are the conditions under which a damaged tip is most likely to break and a repair can do the most good. If there is a question in my mind about the seriousness of a nick, scratch, or scrape in one of my own rods, I'm inclined to fix it rather than face more serious consequences later.

After examining the shaft and flagging any damage that needs attention, inspect the female ferrule or ferrules. This is particularly important if your rod sections tend to separate when you are fishing or casting; such a problem is generally traceable to a cracked ferrule. Again, using a magnifying glass, look at the rim of the ferrule, checking for any chips or visible cracks; cracks typically appear as small white lines across the lip of the ferrule or running lengthwise down the shaft. Then join two sections of the rod. Bend the rod shaft between your hands so it flexes at the ferrule; again, inspect the edge of the female ferrule. Some small cracks won't be visible unless they are widened under stress. Rotate the shaft slightly, flex the rod again, and examine a new section of the ferrule edge, continuing until you've examined the entire perimeter.

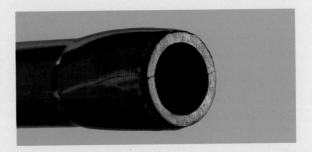

The ferrule shown here has two cracks—a larger one on the near side and a smaller one on the far side. This ferrule will be reinforced in the sequence shown on pages 32–36. If you detect a crack in the ferrule, don't fish the rod until the repair is made. Damage like this only gets worse.

Next, check the guides individually. On saltwater rods particularly, be alert for signs of corrosion.

Corrosion on guides typically begins in the small hollow under the guide frame where the foot meets the thread wraps, as shown here, or on welds or corners of stripping guides. Notice that the finish over the thread wraps is cracked. Water has entered beneath the wraps, and you can see rust beginning to appear at the toe of the guide as well. This guide should be replaced.

Look also for guides that have been twisted or bent, even if only slightly. The inside area of a snake guide is not large, and any deformation of the wire can make it smaller still, which restricts the fly line during casting. Check as well for any guides that are loose; wiggle them with your fingers, both crosswise to the blank and along its axis, testing for any sliding or slippage of the guide feet beneath the thread wraps, especially on guides that have been bent or twisted. Inspect the finish over the thread wraps; if it's cracked or crazed, it may signal that the guide foot has broken free beneath it. A guide that is severely bent or shows signs of corrosion should be replaced. A guide that is loose, but otherwise in good condition, should be rewrapped; if a loose guide has too much play beneath the thread wrap, the guide foot can chisel into the rod shaft and produce a weak spot.

On trout rods, wear or grooving of the guides from line abrasion is rarely a problem. But on saltwater rods, it can occur, particularly on rods used for bigger species such as tarpon, or when small-diameter, gel-spun poly fly-line backing is used. Inspect each guide for wear or run a small piece of nylon stocking material through each guide; it will snag on any burrs or rough spots that might damage fly line.

Check the tip-top for these same problems—bent wire, looseness, wear, or rough spots. Then sight down the tip section of the rod to make sure that the tip-top hasn't rotated out of alignment with the rest of the guides.

Next, inspect the grip for any gouges or tears in the cork, or pieces of cork that have broken from the front or rear edge of the grip. (I once had a grip that needed extensive patching after it had been nibbled by mice.) For the most part, repairs to the cork are a matter of cosmetics, though a rough spot on the cork that falls beneath your thumb or fingers can be an annoyance.

Finally, check the butt cap of the rod to make sure it is tightly glued. Just firmly grip the cap, pull and twist, and test for any looseness or play. A solidly mounted butt cap is especially crucial on downlocking reel seats—where the locking rings screw toward the butt of the rod—since the butt cap has a hood that holds the reel foot. If the butt cap comes loose on the water, your rod and reel will quickly part ways. On uplocking seats—where the locking rings screw toward the rod tip—or on sliding-ring-type seats, the butt cap doesn't help secure the reel, but it does prevent the locking rings and hood from sliding off the end of the rod.

ROD REPAIRS

I hate to begin this section with bad news, but generally speaking there is really no good way to repair a rod shaft that has been crushed or broken. It may be possible, at least in some cases, to repair such damage by using a sleeve or splint, either inside of or over the break, to join the sections together. But this approach, in my experience, has never been very satisfactory. Finding a properly sized sleeve or splint requires a stockpile of spare rod-shaft material that most of us simply don't have. Tip breakage is far and away the most common type, and repairing a broken tip with an external sleeve adds so much weight to the forward portion of the rod that a disappointing change in the action is usually the result. And perhaps most importantly, splints and sleeves made of hollow rod-shaft material often don't hold, and the rod ends up breaking again—at no small cost in time and effort. Theoretically, it should be possible to mend rod sections with a stronger internal sleeve of the solid graphite used to make spigot ferrules. But this material is not commercially available, and even if it were, getting a precise fit for a strong repair could be difficult. The most viable option with a broken rod is to contact the manufacturer for a replacement section. If, however, the damage occurs relatively close to the tip of the rod, you may be able to trim away the damage and mount a new tip-top as explained later in this section.

Fortunately, repairs to less catastrophic damage are quite feasible and usually successful. But before undertaking any repairs on a rod still under warranty, it is worth checking with the manufacturer to determine if the damage falls under the terms of the warranty or to see if effecting the repair yourself will compromise the warranty. In this case, you may wish to have the repair done by the manufacturer. For rods no longer under warranty, or for emergency field repairs, this precaution is of course not an issue.

REPAIRING ROD-SHAFT DAMAGE

It's not necessary to repair scratches or nicks that damage only the finish on a rod; these have no effect on the structural integrity. But if aesthetics are important to you, you may be able to remove light scratches with a rubbing or scratch-removing compound used for automobiles. Blemishes that can't be buffed out can usually be hidden by using a commercially available rod finish such as Perma Gloss. Note that this type of finish is different from the compound used to varnish the thread wraps on guides. It is much lighter and thinner, and you may want to thin it even further in order to apply just a light film over the damage so that the finish blends with the rest of the rod shaft.

Nicks or scratches in the shaft that go deeper than the exterior finish can be repaired, at least much of the time. It is certainly possible that damage to the tiny filaments of graphite or fiberglass that make up the shaft is so severe that, eventually, breakage is inevitable. By the same token, nothing is lost by attempting a repair, particularly since, as noted earlier, it can be difficult to determine how extensive the damage actually is.

Repairs of this type are made by reinforcing the damaged area with thread and applying a finish to the thread wraps, in very much the same way that the guides are mounted on a rod. Conventional rod-wrapping thread can certainly be used for these repairs, and it does have two advantages—it is relatively easy to work with, and, if aesthetics are a concern, the thread color can be chosen to match the rest of the wrappings on the rod. If you opt for conventional thread, make sure it is rod-wrapping thread, not nylon or polyester fly-tying thread or sewing thread. Fly-tying threads are often waxed, and the wax may prevent the adhesion of the finish given to the finished wraps. By the same token, some sewing threads are treated with silicone to slide more easily through sewing-machine mechanisms, and this treatment can be incompatible with some finishes. If the finished appearance of the repair is a high priority and you wish to use rod-wrapping thread, see additional details about these threads in the section "Replacing a Guide," page 27.

While rod-wrapping thread is practical for reinforcing a damaged shaft, a stronger and lighter repair, particularly in the more fragile tip section of the rod, can be achieved by using a stronger type of thread. Aramid fibers—a family of very lightweight, high-strength nylon fibers—are especially well suited to the task, and indeed such fibers are sometimes used in the actual construction of the rod. The best-known member of this family is Kevlar, used to make body armor and bulletproof vests. It may sound a little exotic, but Kevlar is in fact readily, and inexpensively, available in the form of thread used by fly tyers—an ideal format for our purposes here. The thread is suitably sized for many rod repairs and a standard item in most fly shops. You must, however, make sure the thread is unwaxed. Note that Kevlar thread is available in only one color, a pale yellow. It turns slightly translucent when finish is applied over the thread wraps, which may or may not be cosmetically pleasing, if that matters to you.

An alternative to Kevlar, and the one I prefer, is gel-spun polyethylene (GSP) thread. This fiber is a popular material for lines in the general fishing market because of its extremely high strength, low stretch, and small diameter, and it is sometimes favored as fly-line backing by saltwater anglers who need very high backing capacities for very large fish such as tarpon or billfish. Like Kevlar, GSP is available in the form of fly-tying thread, and in fact it has a couple of advantages over Kevlar. While Kevlar is not an especially thick thread (if you tie flies, it's typically about 200 denier, or approximately the equivalent of size 3/0 tying thread), it may seem a little bulky for repairs on thin tip sections of the rod. GSP thread is available in more sizes—a 50 denier (about the equivalent of 12/0 tying thread); 100 denier (about a 7/0 thread); 130 denier (about 6/0 thread), and 180 denier (roughly 3/0). This range of sizes allow a low-profile, high-strength repair to almost any portion of the rod. And while, as of this writing, GSP thread is available in only one color—white—the thread wraps become partially transparent once finish is applied. If you choose to reinforce the rod with gel-spun polyethylene, make sure to use fly-tying thread, not commercially available fishing line. Some of these lines have chemical coatings and additives that may prevent varnish adhesion.

The photograph in Step 5, page 25, shows rod-wrapping thread, Kevlar, and GSP both with and without varnish to give you an idea of how the finished wraps appear in comparison with the thread on the spool.

Kevlar and GSP threads do share a couple of drawbacks, though in my estimation they are slight compared with the virtues. They are quite slippery and not quite as easy to work with as ordinary rod-wrapping thread, and the fibers are so tough that they are difficult to cut cleanly with scissors. Moreover, these threads are not round in cross section. They are more ribbonlike (if you tie flies, they are "flat" threads), and wrapping them smoothly and consistently takes a bit more attention. Their use is demonstrated on pages 33–36.

There's no hard-and-fast rule about a suitable thread size for reinforcing a rod shaft, but as a general guideline, if you go with rod-wrapping thread, choose size A for tip sections, and the thicker, stronger size D for middle and butt sections of the rod. For repairs to portions of the shaft about 1/16 inch in diameter or less, go with

50- or 100-denier GSP thread; for butt sections, Kevlar or 180-denier GSP; for the middle portions of the rod, 100- to 180-denier GSP or Kevlar thread.

Finally, if you have access to them, a couple of pieces of equipment can simplify the job—a rod-wrapping stand and a motorized rod turner; many fly shops have these available for use or loan as a service to their customers. But they are merely conveniences, not necessities. The modified cardboard box shown in the following instructions works perfectly well.

Here's what you'll need:
- A cardboard box as shown below
- Two heavy books—dictionaries or thick phone directories, for instance
- A coffee cup
- A sharp single-edged razor blade
- A 10-inch length of 5X or 6X tippet material

Here's the procedure for a reinforcing repair to a damaged shaft, and in fact, these instructions are the foundation for other types of thread-based repairs explained later in this chapter. One suggestion for all of these repairs: If getting a cosmetically pleasing appearance is a high priority with you, practice wrapping thread on a piece of wooden dowel or, if you have one, a scrap of rod blank. A few trial runs should familiarize you with the thread handling.

STEP 1: You can make a wrapping stand to support the rod from a cardboard box. It should be at least 12 inches wide to give working space for your hands. With a utility knife, cut V notches in the sides. The point of the V should be about 3 to 4 inches from the bottom of the box in order to position your hands at a comfortable working height, and the notches should be symmetrical so that the rod is level

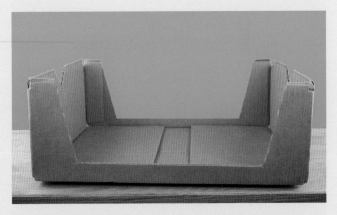

when cradled in them. Leave a perimeter of cardboard at the corners, as shown here, to give the box some rigidity.

STEP 2: Here's a side view of the setup. To wrap this rod, you'd be sitting at the right with the shaft crosswise in front of you.

Put the thread spool in the coffee cup. Strip off about 18 inches of thread and run it between the middle pages of a book placed behind the box. Sandwiching the thread between the pages puts tension on it. Pull on the thread. The thread tension should be quite firm, but not excessively tight. If the tension is too light, put one or more books on top of the first to put more pressure on the thread as it comes through the pages. If the tension is too tight, slip the thread between pages closer to the top of the book to reduce the pressure on it. Place a second heavy book inside the cardboard box to give it some weight and stability.

Make sure the area on the shaft to be repaired is clean—you can use a little rubbing alcohol if necessary—and completely dry. Cradle the rod in the notches so that the area to be repaired is centered in the working field.

Rod-wrapping thread is used here for greater visibility in the demonstration. If you're using Kevlar or GSP, see pages 33–36 for information about handling these threads.

STEP 3: You can make this reinforcement wrap in either direction, wrapping to your left or to your right. We'll be going right to left in this demonstration. To begin wrapping, take the tag of thread. Bring it over the top of the shaft, all the way around the rod, ending with tag pulled toward you, as shown. This first wrap should be positioned ¼ to ½ inch beyond the edge of the damaged area.

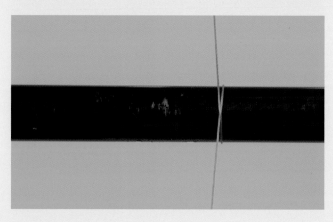

STEP 4: Put some tension on the thread tag with your right fingers. With your left index finger, gently lift the spool thread and move it to the left, so that it crosses the tag thread, as shown. If a little slack develops in the thread, pull the tag in your right fingers to snug the thread against the rod.

STEP 5: The object of the first few wraps is to use the spool thread to pin the thread tag against the rod shaft so that the wrappings won't unravel.

Place the tip of your left thumb right on top of the shaft where the two threads cross, and press firmly as shown. In the next step, you'll roll the rod, and you must have enough thumb pressure to prevent the thread from slipping as you rotate the shaft.

STEP 6: With your right hand, roll the rod shaft toward you (that is, counterclockwise if you were sighting down the rod from the right end). As you begin rolling, press in with your left thumb to keep the thread from sliding. Thread will be pulled from the spool onto the rod, making a second wrap; try to keep

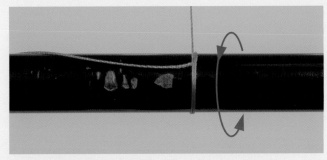

this thread wrap as close to the first one as possible. As you roll, your left thumb will travel to the underside of the shaft. When it gets there, stop rolling for a moment, and carefully slide your thumb over the thread back to the top of the shaft, maintaining pressure as you do so. Then continue rolling until the second wrap crosses the thread tag, as shown here.

STEP 7: Repeat Steps 5 and 6 two more times, taking a third and fourth wrap as close as possible to the previous ones. The tag should be secure enough that you no longer need to hold it with your thumb.

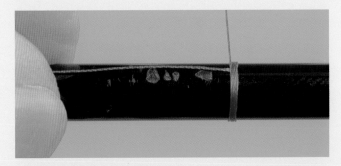

STEP 8: Clip away the excess thread tag. Continue rolling the rod, laying each wrap precisely beside the previous one, covering the clipped end of the thread tag. Here, the wraps have reached to about the middle of the repair area.

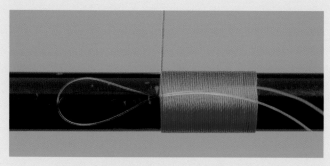

STEP 9: Continue wrapping until you are about five or six thread wraps' distance from the end of the repair, which is ¼ to ½ inch beyond the edge of the damaged area. Maintain tension on the thread; you can rest the heels of your hands on the shaft to prevent any slack from developing. Take the piece of tippet material, and fold it in half. Slip it down behind the wrapping thread so that it is pinned against the blank and held in position. Note that the loop end of the tippet points away from the damaged section.

STEP 10: Continue wrapping, binding the monofilament loop against the rod shaft, until the damaged area is approximately centered in the band of thread wraps. Press your left thumb against the thread wraps to keep tension on them. With your right hand, clip the thread about 2 inches beyond the tip of your thumb. Then insert the clipped thread through the loop as shown.

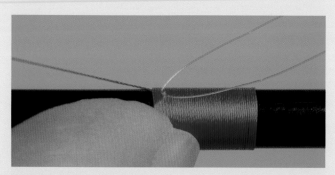

STEP 11: Maintain pressure on the thread wraps with your left thumb. Use your right hand to pull the tag ends of the tippet material. As the loop is drawn under the thread wraps, it will pull the thread tag along with it.

STEP 12: Continue pulling the ends of the tippet until the tag of thread emerges completely from beneath the thread wraps. Tension will now hold the thread tag, and the wraps will not unravel.

STEP 13: With your left fingers, raise the thread tag vertically. With your right hand, use the razor blade to trim off the thread tag as closely as possible to the thread wraps. Be extremely careful not to nick the wrappings with the razor blade.

Now you're ready to apply the finish as shown in the next section.

VARNISHING THREAD WRAPS

To complete a repair that requires new thread wraps, you must use rod-wrapping finish to secure the wraps in place and prevent them from unraveling, to seal out moisture, and generally to protect them from damage. (Rod builders often refer to this finish generically as "varnish"—a throwback to earlier days when that was the finish of choice. Virtually no modern graphite or fiberglass production rods use true varnish as thread-wrap finish, but the term persists.) There are a variety of such finishes available in fly shops that carry rod-building supplies and from outfits that specialize in components for the home rod builder. Probably the most practical type for repairs are the two-part finishes that will do the job in one coat (these are sometimes called "high build" finishes). Typically, the finish components come supplied with measuring syringes, since getting the mixture proportions of the two materials is crucial to a finish that dries hard. But there are also one-part, no-mix finishes that will certainly do the job; they may just require more than one coat.

If you wish to maintain the original color of the rod-wrapping thread, you'll need to apply a color preserver. Color preserver is a thin sealant that prevents the rod-wrapping finish from soaking into the thread and changing its color. The photograph in Step 5 gives an idea of how color preserver and rod-wrapping finish affect the color of the thread.

You'll also need one or more brushes to apply the finish; the inexpensive kind sold by the dozen for schoolchildren are just fine. Or individual disposable brushes are available from rod-building suppliers or hobby stores.

To finish the new thread wraps, you'll need:
- Color preserver (if desired)
- Rod finish

- Aluminum foil
- Toothpicks or a sandwich-size plastic bag for mixing the finish
- A drinking straw or hollow plastic coffee stirrer
- Small disposable paintbrush (two, if using color preserver)

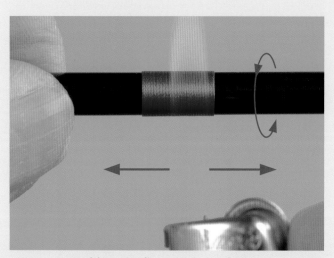

STEP 1: You can improve the appearance of the finished wraps with a little surface preparation. The frayed end of the trimmed thread and the little fuzzy fibers on the wrappings that come from a slight abrasion as the thread is drawn may cause tiny bumps or unevenness in the rod-wrapping finish. You can remove them with a butane lighter if you are careful.

Light the flame. Hold the rod so that the thread wraps are to the side of the flame, about ½ to ¼ inch away. Move the flame back and forth across the thread wraps as you rotate the rod; the heat will singe off any fuzz.

The keys points here are (a) don't get the flame too close or you can scorch or burn the thread; (b) keep the flame moving so one portion of the wraps doesn't get too hot; and (c) always keep the thread wraps alongside the flame, not above it.

STEP 2: If you've used rod-wrapping thread, you may want to apply color preserver. Color preserver is fairly simple to apply; just brush it on as you would apply rod-wrapping finish, as shown in Steps 3 and 4. Brush it on in a thin coat; when you're finished, use the brush to pop any small bubbles that appear. There's no need to rotate the blank as the color preserver dries. Most color preservers require two or more coats to completely seal the thread, and each coat should be completely dry before applying the next. When the final coat is dry, you can apply the rod-wrapping finish.

The procedure for applying the finish is the same whether color preserver is used or not. If you're using a two-part finish, measure and mix it according to the instructions. Here are a few tips.

- Work in a room where the temperature is at least 70 degrees. Two-part finishes give the best results when they are warmer. You can gently heat the two finish components by immersing the bottles or syringes in warm water for about 10 minutes prior to mixing.
- Measure the two components carefully. Use syringes. If they weren't supplied with the finish you bought, you can get measuring syringes at a hobby store or from a rod-building supplier. Don't use medical syringes; they can contain lubricants that may damage the finish.
- Though varnishing the thread wraps may take only a very small amount of finish, mix more than you need—3 to 4 cc (or about a teaspoon) for an average repair. Small errors in measuring the proportions of the two compounds become less significant when the total volume of the material is greater, and the handling or curing properties of the finish won't be affected.

There are a few different approaches to mixing:
- Dispense the two components onto a square of aluminum foil, and mix them thoroughly with a toothpick or stirring stick.
- Some finishes are sold in kits that contain small plastic mixing cups and stirring sticks. These work fine. After mixing the finish, pour it into an aluminum foil tray.
- Or you can use this method, shown to me by the owner of a hobby store. Cut the corner from a plastic sandwich bag to make a cone 3 to 4 inches tall. Carefully dispense the components into the corner of the bag. Twist the bag to make a little pouch, and knead the mixture for two minutes. Then snip the tip from the corner, and squeeze the finish into a foil tray.

In all three of these methods, the finish ends up on the square of foil, as shown in the photo, for a couple of reasons. First, spreading the finish out extends its working life. Second, mixing introduces bubbles into the finish (though the plastic-bag method minimizes bubbles), and these bubbles can be carried to the thread wraps and dry there. It doesn't hurt anything—it's just a cosmetic matter—but just a bit of attention will produce a neater, more attractive job. Let the finish sit in the foil tray for a minute or two. Bubbles will form or rise on the surface. You can break them by gently blowing on them through a straw. There's no need to be obsessive about it—some bubbles will probably be transferred to the thread wraps anyway—but getting rid of some of them now simplifies things later.

If you're using a cheap disposable brush to apply the finish, you may find that the bristle tips are ragged and uneven, and some bristles splay to the side, as shown on the brush at the bottom in Step 2. Neatening up the brush will give a better finish. Lay the brush on a block of wood, and use a single-edged razor to slice across the bristle tips and square them off, as shown on the brush at the top; if any bristles splay to the side, cut them off the near the ferrule of the brush.

STEP 3: The easiest way to apply the finish is to rotate the blank, letting the thread wraps pull finish from the brush. Pick up a drop of finish on the brush. Touch it to the thread near one end of the wrap, and begin turning the rod shaft. As this section of the wrapping gets coated with finish, slide the brush toward the end of the thread wrap, pushing a bead of finish over the outermost wrap of thread and onto the rod shaft. You want to seal this last wrap with a band of finish that extends about ½₂ inch onto the shaft.

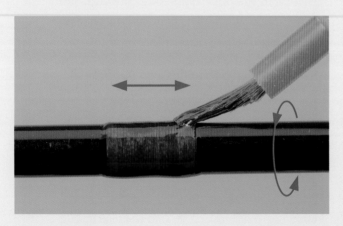

STEP 4: Pick up additional drops of finish and apply them to the thread wraps. You want to apply enough finish to completely cover the thread wraps in a smooth coat, but not encase them in an overly thick gob of finish. After the wraps are coated, keep the rod turning, and work the tip of the brush back and forth over the top of the finish to level it out across the wraps as evenly as possible.

STEP 5: After the finish is applied, it's necessary to rotate the rod so that the viscous finish doesn't sag to one side of the shaft and dry there as a big hump. If you're using a motorized turner, just mount the rod and turn it on. If you're using a cardboard box, you'll have to rotate it by hand. You don't need to keep the rod turning continuously, however. Rather, give the rod a quarter turn every 10 or 15 minutes for the next 90 minutes or so. (I usually set a cooking timer, and attend to the rod while I'm reading or watching TV.)

Inspect the finish every few minutes for the first 20 to 30 minutes. If bubbles appear, blow on them through a straw to break them. If you're careful, you can also use a butane lighter to break them, using exactly the same approach you took in Step 1 to singe the wraps. Slowly bring the side of the flame toward the bubble until it breaks. After the finish sets up, you don't need to rotate the rod anymore, though if it's in a motorized turner, there's no harm in doing so. Let the finish cure for about 24 hours.

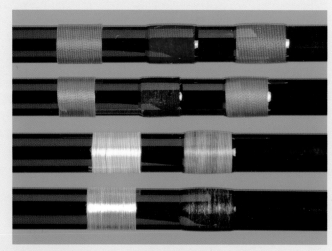

Shown at the top left is a wrap similar to the one made in this sequence, with no finish applied. Next to it is a wrap that has been varnished, but no color preserver applied. Note how the color darkens when the varnish soaks into the thread. At the top right is a wrap that was given three coats of color preserver and then varnished; the original thread color is closely maintained. The green wraps in the second row have been treated like those in the top row to show the effects of rod-wrapping finish and color preserver on a different color of thread. In the third row, an unfinished Kevlar wrapping is at the left. A similar wrap on the right has had finish applied; note the slight translucence. On the bottom row, an unfinished GSP wrap is shown at left. The GSP wrap on the right has been varnished; notice how the wraps become partially transparent.

The light and dark bands on the Kevlar and GSP threads occur because these flat threads spread and lay down almost like ribbon; it's difficult to wind them on the shaft in neat, edge-to-edge wraps. Instead, there is some overlap, and where the wraps overlap, they appear more opaque.

REMOVING OLD THREAD WRAPS

Some repairs, such as replacing a guide or reinforcing a cracked ferrule, require that existing thread wraps first be removed. The challenge here is taking off the old varnish that coats the wraps. Two-part finishes in particular can be a little tricky to remove. One experienced rod-repair person advised the following method, and I've found it to work very well. The idea here is to apply lacquer thinner to the thread wraps and let it stand long enough to soften the old finish. At the same time, you want to minimize contact with the rod itself or the solvent may remove the surface finish on the shaft. If some of the rod finish is removed, the only harm is cosmetic. And in fact if the rod finish is removed or marred on the area that will be subsequently wrapped with thread, no harm at all is done since that section of the shaft will be concealed.

Here's what you'll need to strip off the old thread wraps:

- Strips of cotton cloth, such as pieces cut from an old T-shirt
- Lacquer thinner (acetone will also work)
- Aluminum foil
- Some wooden Popsicle-type sticks
- Rags
- Single-edged razor blade
- Latex gloves
- A well-ventilated work space safely distant from any source of open flame or sparks; lacquer thinner (and acetone) fumes are strong, and the solvent is quite volatile

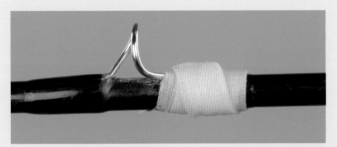

STEP 1: Cut a strip of cotton cloth about one-quarter to one-half the width of the thread wrap you are trying to remove and long enough to wrap around the repair area in slightly overlapping turns from one end of the varnished area to another. Put on the latex gloves and dip the strip in lacquer thinner. Squeeze out the excess so that the strip is almost saturated, but not wringing wet. Carefully wrap the cloth around the thread wraps you wish to remove. Confine the strip as much as possible to the varnished area only, as shown here; don't wrap the cloth around the shaft itself. The wetness of the strip will hold it in place.

STEP 2: Immediately after wrapping the cloth, cover the area with aluminum foil to prevent the solvent from evaporating during its contact time with the varnished wraps. Here, both feet on the guide have been wrapped in solvent-soaked strips and overwrapped with foil.

STEP 3: The timing is a bit of a balancing act. You want to give the solvent enough time to soften the existing finish, but not enough to work its way down to the finish on the rod blank itself beneath the thread. Try about 15 minutes to start with. Then remove the foil and the cloth strips. If the finish feels tacky or looks pocked, pitted, or dulled, you're ready to go.

With a wooden stick or piece of plastic (but not a metal tool of any kind), begin scraping the softened finish from the thread wraps. It may come off as a slightly gummy residue, or it may scrape off as a sticky, fine, whitish powder, as shown here. Work around the rod shaft, removing all the soft material until you are scraping against the surface of the thread itself.

If not all the finish has softened, and there are still spots of hard finish over parts of the thread, repeat Steps 1 and 2 again, applying more lacquer thinner. But let it work for a shorter time, perhaps five minutes or so.

STEP 4: When you've removed the finish down to the thread wraps, very carefully cut the first few thread wraps at one end of the wrapping with a razor blade. Peel away the cut tags of thread until you have a single thread strand that is still attached to the rod. Pull this thread, letting the rod spin, until you have removed the entire wrapping.

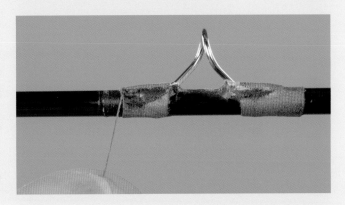

STEP 5: Remove the guide. You will see some ridges of old finish created by the thread wraps and probably a thicker buildup of old finish that accumulated beneath the guide wire, as shown at the left. The thick buildup can be difficult to remove with solvent alone. Use a very sharp knife, like an X-Acto

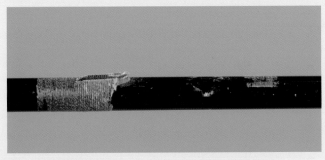

type, to remove some of this excess finish. Work parallel to the rod shaft to avoid nicking it. Just shave away the high spot—don't try to remove all the old varnish—and then wrap the area in another thin strip of cloth and solvent, letting it work for just a couple of minutes. You should be able to cleanly scrape away any remaining finish. The wrapping shown at the right is nearly done; a little more scraping will clean it up nicely. With a little patience, you can completely strip off the old finish right down to the shaft and leave a smooth foundation for the new thread wraps.

REPLACING A GUIDE

If you're rewrapping an existing guide, you'll already have a guide of the proper size at hand. If you're replacing a guide, you'll need to obtain a new guide of the same size, or at least close to it. Guides are available at fly shops that stock rod-building materials, and many rod-building suppliers have paper or online catalogs that contain life-size silhouette drawings of snake guides. You should be able to compare the damaged guide to the illustration to find the correct size.

You need to select a thread as well, and as noted earlier, don't use fly-tying thread or ordinary sewing thread; these may be treated with materials that can inhibit a clean finish on the wraps. Rod-wrapping thread comes in various sizes, but practically speaking, size A thread can be used to wrap virtually any guide on any fly rod. Extreme strength is not required; the cumulative pressure of the many thread wraps under moderate tension does the job. The one possible exception here is wrapping a large guide on the thick butt section of a heavy rod; you may wish to use size D thread, not because it is stronger, but because the thicker thread diameter wraps more quickly over large areas.

In buying thread, you may also be confronted with a decision between two types. The first is ordinary rod-wrapping thread. When varnish is applied to this type of thread, it will change color to some extent, as shown on page 25; the thread becomes darker and more translucent, and brighter colors become more muted. Some people prefer this effect, and if it appeals to you or matches the wraps on the rest of your rod, by all means go this route. If you want to maintain more closely the color of the thread as it appears on the spool, you can treat the thread wraps with color preserver, a thin prefinish that seals in the thread color. The thread will still darken a bit, but brighter colors will stay brighter, again as shown on page 25, and most thread colors will remain more opaque.

The alternative to ordinary thread is a type that requires no color preserver. These threads are usually identified as NCP (no color preserver) thread or PNR (preserver not required) thread. After wrapping these threads, you can start directly on the finish coat.

If getting a good color match with the rest of your rod wraps is important, you may want to buy the two or three spools of thread of colors that most closely resemble the original. Thread is relatively inexpensive, and it's never entirely obvious what color the thread will end up once it's varnished. Wrap short bands of thread around a dowel or scrap of rod blank, apply finish to see how the final color appears, and choose the best match.

Guides on many rods are wrapped with two colors—a main thread color used to secure the guide, and a thin band of a second color; this second color is just a trim wrap to enhance the appearance. Since we're concerned with tackle maintenance and repair, the finer points of nonessential aesthetic touches at this level of detail are really beyond the scope of this book. However, if you wish to apply a trim wrap, the procedure is essentially the same as that shown in Steps 3–13 on pages 18–21. The tricky part is that the trim often consists of a just a few wraps of thread. As you begin wrapping the trim, you need to capture the thread tag with only one or two thread wraps, and then immediately mount the loop of tippet material that is used to pull the final tag of thread beneath the wraps. There's a lot going on in a short amount of space. It's not terribly difficult, but a little practice will go a long way in producing a neat job on the rod.

To mount the new guide, you'll need:

- All the materials listed on page 17
- A new guide (if you are replacing an existing one)
- A sharp, flat file (if you're mounting a brand-new guide); an electric grinding wheel or a small handheld grinder such as a Dremel tool will also work
- Masking tape

Here's the procedure:

STEP 1: You must first remove the old guide, but before doing so, take two measurements. First, measure the distance between the center of the guide and the rod ferrule. Write it down so that you can wrap the new guide in the right spot. Second, measure the length from the toe end of the guide to the outermost thread wrap, and write it down as well. When you mount the new guide, you will want to reproduce the length of this original wrapping.

Remove the old guide and the rod-wrapping finish as explained in "Removing Old Thread Wraps," page 25.

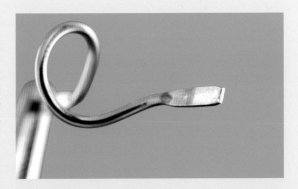

STEP 2: If you're mounting a brand-new guide, look at it closely. Notice, as shown here, that the guide feet are squared off and thick at the toe, so you'll need to do a little preparation. Shaping the feet to make a smooth transition to the rod shaft greatly simplifies wrapping and produces a neater job. (If you're remounting an existing guide, this prep work will already be done, and you can skip to Step 5.)

STEP 3: You can use a sharp file to shape the feet. Very small guides can be difficult to grip with your fingers; hold them in a pair of needle-nose pliers, but wrap the jaws in electrician's tape to prevent marring the guide. An electric grinding tool can be used instead, but work carefully, removing only small amounts of material at a time. Electric tools cut quickly, and it's easy to get carried away.

Round the top of the foot from side to side, making a smooth curve over the top. Then taper the toe of the guide foot, forming a smooth "ramp" over which to wrap the thread. Finally, round the tip of the toe slightly to remove any sharp corners. The finished guide foot is shown here.

Filing or grinding can produce burrs at the edges and toe of the foot, and they can scratch the rod shaft if not removed. Feel the underside of the foot with your finger. If there are any rough edges, stroke them very lightly with a file to smooth them out. Don't use much pressure or you may produce another burr. Or you can set the guide feet flat against a fine sharpening stone, such as a hard Arkansas stone, and lap them lightly to remove any roughness.

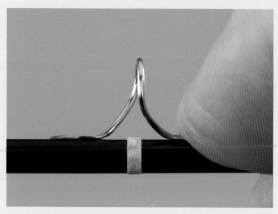

STEP 4: Once the guide is prepared, cut a thin strip of masking tape and wrap it around the rod shaft at the point where the center of the new guide will be located, as shown. You measured this location in Step 1.

Test-fit the guide against the rod. The guide feet should sit flat against the shaft, as shown here. If the feet don't rest flush against the shaft, use a pair of needle-nose pliers, with the jaws wrapped in tape, to straighten the feet. A guide with "splayed" feet, where the toes tip upward, is very difficult to wrap. A guide that rests on the tips of the toes can chisel into the rod shaft under thread pressure and cause a weak spot.

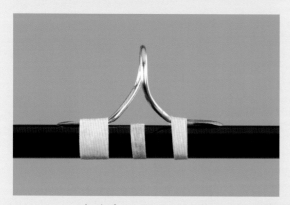

STEP 5: Use additional thin strips of masking tape to mount the guide on the shaft. The center of the guide should lie directly over the strip of tape used in Step 4 to mark the position of the original guide. The tape strips holding the guide itself should be placed at the inside edges of the foot. Since the thread wraps attaching the guide start beyond the toe and move inward, you need enough length of bare foot to cover with thread before removing the tape.

And of course, mount the guide so that it is aligned with the rest of the guides on the rod section. Get the best alignment you can, but you don't need to be perfect. After the guide is taped in place, you can adjust its position slightly. And in fact once the thread wraps are in place, you'll have one more opportunity to fine-tune the alignment.

STEP 6: The procedure for wrapping the guide is identical to that shown in Steps 3–13, pages 18–21. But there are a few details worth noting. First, use a moderate thread tension; you want the wraps to be fairly snug, but tight pressure is not needed. Second, begin wrapping the thread at a distance beyond the toe of the guide that you measured in Step 1; the length of the thread wraps on the new guide will then be properly sized to match those on the rest of the

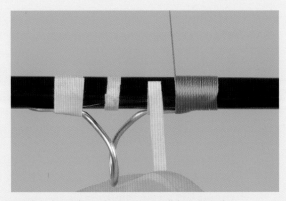

rod. Third, when you wrap toward the guide, wrap the thread as close as possible up to the toe of the guide. Then make the next wrap carefully; it's the first one that will "climb up" the toe of the guide. When making the wrap, keep the thread squared up to the rod shaft and make the wrap as seamless looking as possible, as shown here.

Once you've wrapped over about half the foot, it will be secure enough so that you can remove the tape, as shown.

STEP 7: As you approach the end of the guide foot, bind in the loop of tippet material that will be used to help secure the wraps; the tippet loop points away from the toe of the guide. Make sure that the loop is bound to a part of shaft that is well away from the guide. There is a small hollow space beneath the thread on each side of the guide foot. If you mount the tippet loop too close to this space and pull the thread tag through the hollow beneath the wraps, there may not be enough tension to hold the tag in place, and the thread will unravel.

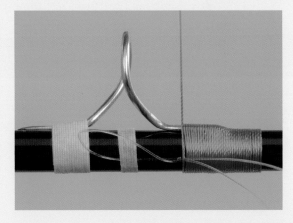

STEP 8: Here's the completed guide wrapping. At this point, sight down the rod blank to make sure the new guide is aligned with the others. If it's not, adjust its position. Rather than pulling on the guide ring, use your thumbnail to push against the side of one foot. Move it just a short distance; then adjust the position of the other foot so that the guide again lies along the axis of the rod shaft. Work in short increments rather than

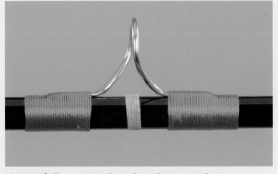

trying to adjust the position all at once. And work carefully; remember that the wrappings are not yet coated with finish. You don't want to fray them with your thumbnail or spread the wraps apart.

At this point, you can apply finish to the wraps as described in "Varnishing Thread Wraps," page 21.

LOOSE FERRULE

According to a repair expert I spoke with, most ferrules that persistently loosen during fishing are actually cracked, and that repair is explained in the next section. But if, after close inspection, you feel that the female ferrule is intact, the looseness probably results from an improper fit of the male ferrule, which has worn down over time; the edge of the female ferrule is not seating tightly against the surface of the male end.

You may be able to remedy the problem by building up the diameter of the male end of the ferrule with a thin coat of hard rod finish such as Perma Gloss. (Note that this is a thin finish used on rod shafts, not the thicker, two-part finish used to varnish thread wraps.) Apply a thin, even coat to the male ferrule, and let it dry. If it's still loose, add another coating, repeating until the ferrule fits snugly. While this type of repair will last for a while, it isn't permanent, ultimately wearing down as you repeatedly assemble and disassemble the rod sections, at which point the coating must be renewed.

CRACKED FERRULE

Like all repairs to the rod shaft, the success in mending a cracked ferrule depends to some degree on the extent of the damage. A female ferrule that has developed a short crack or split at the lip can generally be repaired; a crack that has migrated down the length of the ferrule may be too far gone. There is really only way one to tell—strip off any old thread wraps on the ferrule, assess the damage, then fix it and see if it holds.

A cracked female ferrule can be repaired in much the same way as a deep scratch or nick in the rod shaft—by reinforcing the damaged area with thread wraps. There is one difference, though: There may be a snake guide wrapped at the ferrule as well. For a clean and effective repair, all thread wraps, and the guide if there is one, must be removed as explained on page 25.

Here's what you'll need to repair the ferrule:
- The materials listed on page 17
- Additional books or weight to apply more pressure on the thread
- GSP or Kevlar thread
- Rod-wrapping thread of the desired color if you wish to overwrap the repair for better cosmetics or mount a guide over the repair wraps

Before proceeding, you'll need to decide on the specifics of the repair, which depend partly on aesthetic preferences and partly on the guide placement.

If your rod has no guide at the ferrule and you wish only a simple, workmanlike repair, you can wrap the ferrule area with GSP or Kevlar thread. The repair will be fairly inconspicuous. GSP and Kevlar threads are preferable to nylon rod-wrapping thread; they are much stronger. More importantly, they have very little stretch and will prevent the crack from opening up even when the rod is flexed at the ferrule point. Nylon thread, by comparison, is fairly elastic.

If your rod has no guide at the ferrule and you wish the repair to match the rest of wrappings on the rod, you can wrap the ferrule with a Kevlar or GSP thread base and then overwrap this base with rod-winding thread in the color of your choice.

If your rod has a guide at the ferrule, you can effect the repair with Kevlar or GSP thread and remount the guide with rod-wrapping thread of the desired color over this foundation as shown in "Replacing a Guide," page 27. When the guide is remounted, however, there will be a small band of foundation thread beneath the center of the guide that you won't be able to cover with rod-wrapping thread. If you repair the ferrule with GSP thread, this band will be nearly invisible.

As noted earlier, GSP and Kevlar threads are "flat"; that is, they are made up of many tiny filaments, much like fly-tying floss, that aren't bonded together. Handling these threads is a bit trickier than using rod-wrapping thread. The tiny filaments tend to separate and stray, particularly when wrapping pressure is applied, and keeping the thread confined to a narrow band takes some attention. These threads can also fray as they are handled, leaving small, broken filaments on the thread wrap.

I prefer GSP thread over Kevlar since it is tougher, tends to fray less, and is generally easier to work with. Even so, you won't get a thread wrap that is quite as smooth or uniform in appearance as that produced by rod-wrapping thread. But the repair will be much stronger. GSP thread is used in the following demonstration, but Kevlar thread is handled in the same way.

STEP 1: If your rod has a guide at the ferrule that will need to be removed, measure the distance from the end of the ferrule to the center of the guide, and write it down. When it comes time to replace the guide, you'll want to mount it at the correct location. Then use the

procedure shown in "Removing Old Thread Wraps," page 25, to strip all the thread wraps and old finish from ferrule area and guide feet.

Shown here is the ferrule pictured on page 13, where inspection revealed cracking. The thread wraps over the ferrule have been removed to reveal the extent of the damage; the crack shown here is about ½ inch long.

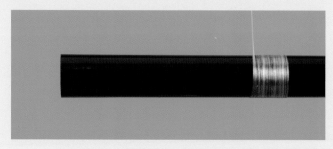

STEP 2: The procedure for reinforcing the ferrule with thread is almost identical to that used for repairing damage to the shaft, as shown previously. But there are a couple of small differences. First, heavier thread tension is used to help draw the crack tightly closed. And second, because the ferrule is at one end of the rod section, you won't be able to center the ferrule between the notches in the box stand; instead, cradle the rod so that the ferrule extends a short distance beyond one end of the box. (Don't join the ferrule with another rod section in order to center the repair area between the notches; joining the sections will simply hold the crack open, and the repair wraps will do little good.)

To begin, use the setup shown in Steps 1 and 2, pages 17–18. Add enough weight on the book supplying thread tension to get a moderately firm pressure. In this repair, the thread will be wrapped toward the end of the ferrule. Wrapping in this direction will allow you to get the thread wraps started more easily using less thread pressure. Once the thread is anchored to the rod shaft, additional tension can be applied to force the crack closed.

Before starting to wrap, roll the end of the thread several times (in one direction only) between your thumb and forefinger. Twisting the thread like this consolidates the tiny filaments and makes it easier to mount the thread on the shaft. The first wrap should begin about ½ inch beyond the end of the crack or at the end of the original thread-wrap area, whichever distance is greater.

Mount the thread as shown in Steps 3–8, pages 18–19. When mounting the thread, cover the tag end with at least five or six wraps; GSP and Kevlar threads are slippery and need extra wraps to secure them. Then trim the tag.

When you've wrapped a thread band about ¼ inch wide, add weight atop the book to increase the thread tension to make it very firm. You want tight wraps over the crack.

STEP 3: At this point, the section of thread you twisted in Step 2 will probably be wrapped on the shaft, and the thread will begin to flatten into a ribbonlike shape. It's difficult to place this ribbon of thread in the precise, edge-to-edge wraps that you can get with ordinary rod-wrapping thread. You can control the width of the thread, at least slightly, by pinching it lightly as shown here, and rolling the rod shaft with one hand. Even then, however, the thread will still flatten, particularly under the increased pressure. Don't worry about it—strength is the object here; overlap the thread wraps slightly, and work for as smooth and consistent a wrap as you can.

STEP 4: When you near the end of the ferrule, mount the tippet loop used to finish the wrap.

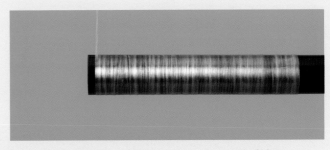

If you are making the repair with GSP thread only, the last thread wrap should be placed about ¹⁄₁₆ inch from the end of the ferrule. You want the thread wraps to cover as much of the ferrule as possible, for strength, and still leave a bit of bare shaft for a small band of varnish when you apply the rod-wrapping finish.

If the rod has a guide at the ferrule, or you intend to overwrap the repair with a rod-wrapping thread that matches the wrappings on the rest of the rod, stop the repair wraps about ⅛ inch from the end of the ferrule, as shown here. This extra space will allow you to place rod-wrapping thread beyond the edge of the repair thread and conceal it.

If a simple repair is all you desire, complete the wrap, and apply rod-wrapping finish as explained in "Varnishing Thread Wraps," page 21.

STEP 5: If you will be remounting a guide at the ferrule or overwrapping this foundation with thread that matches the wraps on the rest of the rod, apply a light coat of rod-wrapping finish to the thread wraps, as shown here. It is certainly possible to mount the guide on a bare, unfinished thread foundation, but if you have very little ex-

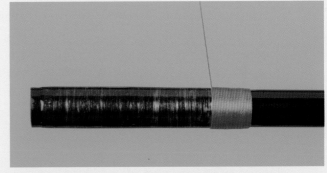

perience wrapping guides, you may find it easier to work over a coat of finish. The finish prevents the guide feet, masking tape used to mount the guide, or new thread wraps from disturbing or damaging the foundation wraps. The key here is to keep the finish thin, and above all, level. You want an even foundation for the next thread wraps. Let this coat dry thoroughly.

To overwrap the foundation with rod-wrapping thread, use the procedure shown in Steps 3-13, pages 18–21. You need only moderate thread tension for the purpose; the rod-wrapping thread is just cosmetic, not structural.

Take the first wrap of thread just at the outside edge of the foundation thread, as shown here, and wrap toward the ferrule end. Take the last wrap of thread just beyond the edge of the foundation thread. Then finish the wraps as explained in "Varnishing Thread Wraps," page 21.

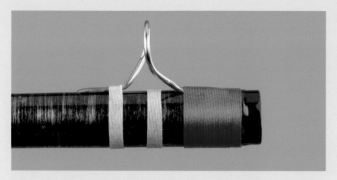

STEP 5A: If you are mounting a guide at the ferrule, use exactly the wrapping procedure shown in "Replacing a Guide," page 27. Then finish the wraps as explained in "Varnishing Thread Wraps," page 21.

BENT OR TWISTED GUIDE

If a snake guide is bent forward or rearward, or twisted sideways, you can simply bend it back to shape if it is not severely deformed. If the guide has been badly crimped and the wire is creased, you may not be able to bend it back to shape, in which case it should be replaced.

The best tool for bending or reshaping a guide is a pair of needle-nose pliers with round, not flat, jaws. Wrap the jaws in electrician's tape to avoid scoring or burring the guide wire, which could damage a fly line later. Work gently to bend the guide back into the proper position; too much force can break the bond between the rod wrapping and the guide foot. If the guide has been pinched so that the line passes through an oval shape rather than a round one, you can insert one of the plier jaws through the guide and re-form the wire by squeezing the pliers, working around the perimeter of the guide wire. Try to bring the guide as nearly as possible back to the original shape so that the fly line passes through the guide with a minimum of friction or interference.

TIP-TOP REPLACEMENT

Replacing a damaged tip-top guide or one that is loose, has twisted out of position, or come off is a simple matter. At least most of the time. It depends on how the original tip-top was affixed to the rod. Many rod manufacturers use a hot glue, such as ferrule cement, for the purpose. This type of glue is easily melted with an ordinary butane lighter, and the tip-top can be removed as shown below. If the tip-top was installed with epoxy, heat will probably still release the bond, though you may need to repeat the heat-and-pull procedure described below several times. If a different adhesive, such as CA glue, was used, this method may not succeed, and you have little recourse but to trim off the tip-top, as shown in the next section ("Broken Rod Tip") and install a new one. You'll lose about ½ inch of the rod tip, but the effect on rod action will be negligible.

If the tip-top is simply loose or has come off the rod, but is otherwise in good shape, you can remount the original hardware. If it's been damaged, you'll need a new one. After removing the tip-top, as shown in Step 1, you can bring the old tip-top to a fly shop that sells rod-building supplies and get one to match. Obviously, the crucial dimension is the inside diameter of the tip-top ferrule—the hole into which the rod tip fits. In the event you have to buy a new tip-top sight unseen, you can measure the old one, but you'll need a finely calibrated ruler or machinist's scale that measures in sixty-fourths of an inch, since that is how tip-tops are usually sized; a "size 4" tip-top, for example, has a ferrule hole $\frac{4}{64}$ inch in diameter.

The new tip-top should slide easily over the rod tip since there needs to be room inside the ferrule for glue. It shouldn't fit too snugly, but by the same token, it shouldn't wobble freely from side to side on the rod tip. If you need to mail order a new tip-top, you might consider purchasing two or three consecutive sizes. They are inexpensive, spares are always good to have, and you'll get the best fit.

The tip-top can be glued with ferrule cement, epoxy, or a gel-type cyanoacrylate glue (such as superglue), though I suggest ferrule cement, which is shown in the following instructions, since it vastly simplifies any future tip-top replacements that might be necessary and the excess glue is easily removed.

For a simple replacement, here's what you need:
- Tip-top of the proper size
- Ferrule cement
- Butane lighter
- Needle-nose pliers

STEP 1: To remove a loose or damaged tip-top, heat it gently and briefly with the side of a butane flame. Then quickly, before the glue rehardens, try to pull off the tip-top with pliers; don't use your fingers, as the metal will be hot. If it doesn't come off, apply a bit more heat and try again until the tip-top slides off.

STEP 2: Use your thumbnail, or a wooden or plastic scraper, to remove the residue of old cement from the rod tip until the surface is clean.

Heat the stick of ferrule cement with the side (not the tip) of a butane flame until the end of stick liquefies and becomes gooey. You may want to roll the stick as you heat it to prevent a drop of the cement from falling off.

Then wipe the end of the cement stick around the rod tip, applying the adhesive to the area that will be covered by the tip-top ferrule. Be fairly generous with the ferrule cement; you want a good bond, and the excess is easily peeled away.

STEP 3: Quickly, while the cement is still pliable, slip the tip-top over the rod shaft. Then sight down the rod, and align the tip-top with the rest of the guides. The excess cement should ooze out from under the ferrule of the tip-top, as shown.

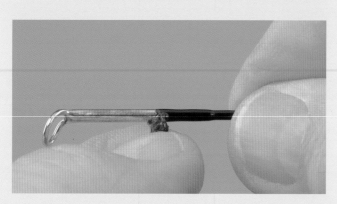

STEP 4: Let the glue cool and harden for a minute or so. Then use your thumbnail to peel away the excess adhesive. Even when dry, ferrule cement is slightly rubbery and elastic and comes off without much trouble.

BROKEN ROD TIP

As noted earlier, there isn't a practical way to rejoin two broken pieces of the rod, but a rod that's broken near the tip may still be salvageable. You can trim the rod just below the break and mount a new tip-top. The success of the repair depends on how near the rod tip the break has occurred and how much change in the casting characteristics of the rod you are willing to tolerate.

A tip broken only an inch or two from the top will almost certainly yield a repaired rod that is at the least satisfactory, and at best very close to the original. Repairing a tip broken more than a few inches down will quite probably affect the rod action, though it may do no more than produce a rod that casts perfectly well but requires one line-weight heavier than the original. A rod broken well into the tip section, say 6 to 8 inches or more, is questionable. Certainly the action and the appropriate line size for the rod will change, but whether the rod is still fishable is a question only the owner can answer. But since the repair is reasonably fast and straightforward, there is no real reason not to try it to see if the rod is still acceptable.

There is one possible circumstance that can complicate matters—if the tip breaks immediately above a snake guide. You may need to remove the guide, thread wraps, and varnish in order to expose enough bare rod tip to install the new tip-top. Or in some cases, after mounting the new tip-top, you may find that the first snake guide is so close to the tip of the rod—say, within an inch—that you might wish to remove it. In a sense, your new, shortened rod now has an extra guide that increases the friction on the line when casting. On a very light fly rod, you may want to eliminate the weight of this extra guide on this thin and sensitive portion of the shaft. The most sensible way to proceed in this case is probably to mount the tip-top, cast the rod, and then decide whether to remove the guide.

Finally, a great many rods have a wrapping of thread just below the tip-top. It's mainly a trim wrap for appearances, but once you cut off the damaged portion and mount the new tip-top, you may want to replace this wrapping. If so, measure the length of the wrapping and write it down so you can duplicate it with new thread. This wrapping is made using exactly the procedure shown in Steps 3–13, pages 18–21.

To trim off the rough or split edge of the broken tip, you'll need:
- An electric hand tool, like a Dremel tool, with an abrasive cutoff wheel (this is the best way to go if you can manage it); or a sharp, fine-toothed triangular file
- 220-grit sandpaper

To mount the new tip-top, you'll need:
- Everything listed on page 37 for "Tip-top Replacement"

STEP 1: For a solid repair, it's important that the tip-top be mounted on an undamaged part of the shaft. Closely inspect the break; using a magnifying glass can help. Even breaks that appear to be clean may in fact have small cracks or splits that run down the shaft. If necessary, insert a needle or toothpick, as shown

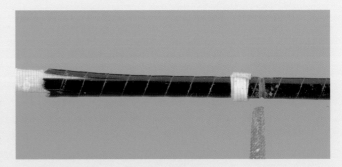

here, into the tip of the rod shaft and apply gentle pressure to open up any cracks very slightly so you can see how far they extend. Don't apply much force or you will split the shaft further. Then use a felt-tipped pen or, as shown here, a strip of masking tape to mark the lowermost point of any damage to the shaft. Though not easily visible in the photograph, the split at the tip of this rod extends down to the tape band. The rod tip will be trimmed off just below this mark.

If you're using a cutoff wheel, simply trim away the damaged portion of the shaft. Rod material cuts easily.

If you're using a triangular file, lay the rod flat on a table or bench. With the corner of the file, make a light cut into the shaft at the cutoff point. Turn the shaft a short way, make another cut, and continue until you have filed a shallow groove around the blank at the cut-off point. Then work your way around the shaft again, making the groove deeper and deeper, as shown here.

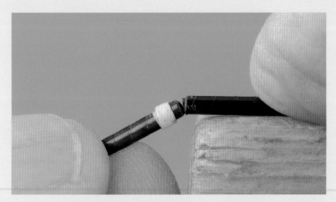

STEP 2: When using a file, you don't actually need to cut all the way through the rod; once the groove is cut well into shaft, lay the rod flat and position the groove at the edge of a tabletop. Snap the broken section off, as shown here. The rod material will shear pretty cleanly. Use the file or sandpaper to clean up any ragged edges or frayed material.

At this point, you'll need to obtain a properly sized tip-top, either by taking the rod section to a fly shop that sells rod-building supplies or by measuring the rod tip, as explained in "Tip-top Repair," and ordering a replacement.

If you find that the new tip end of the rod is so close to a guide that the tip-top won't seat over the tip of the rod, you'll have to remove the guide and varnish as shown in "Removing Old Thread Wraps," page 25.

Once you have the replacement tip-top, very lightly sand the portion of the rod tip that will be covered by the ferrule of the tip-top. You're not trying to remove material—only to rough up the surface a little to give better adhesion to the glue.

Now you can mount the new tip-top using the procedure shown in "Tip-top Replacement," page 36.

STUCK REEL-SEAT LOCKING RINGS

If the screw-locking rings on the reel seat become stuck or frozen up and won't unscrew, the problem may simply be an accumulation of grit caked on the threads. Use warm, soapy water and a stiff-bristled toothbrush to scrub the reel-seat threads at the base of the locking ring. You might need to soak the stuck locking ring for 15 or 20 minutes to let the water penetrate beneath the ring and loosen any dirt there.

If the ring is still stuck, use a penetrating, water-displacement lubricant such as WD-40 or a compound such as Liquid Wrench. Use masking tape to cover a wood reel-seat insert and any rubber components, such as a butt cap, that might be attacked by solvents in the lubricant. Aerosol sprays can be a little messy for close work; instead, spray some of the lubricant into a dish or jar lid. Then use a toothpick or a small paintbrush to apply it to the base of the stuck locking ring. Hold the rod upright so the liquid doesn't drip off and has time to seep between the ring and reel seat. Wait 5 or 10 minutes and apply some more. Then turn the rod upside down and apply some of the lubricant to the other side of the ring. If the ring seems to loosen even a little, continue applying the lubricant to alternate sides of the ring. It should come free.

If the ring is still stuck, it may help to get a better grip to unscrew it; it may be a matter of not getting quite enough torque with your fingers. A pair of channel-lock pliers with the jaws wrapped in duct tape or electrician's tape can help. Be forewarned, however, that at this point we are entering slightly risky territory. To save weight, reel seats are made of thin, and often fairly soft metal, such as aluminum, and they can be easily bent or deformed by the leverage you get with pliers. Adjust the jaw gap so that the jaw faces are as close to parallel as possible when closed on the locking ring. The aim here is only to get a grip on the locking ring, not to squeeze it tightly. The best way to minimize excessive pressure on the locking ring is to grip the ring lightly with the pliers and hold them stationary, concentrating on applying a consistent pressure. With your other hand, turn the cork grip and try to free the ring. If you try to hold the ring and turn the pliers at the same time, the tendency is to tighten your grip as you turn, and you may end up bending the ring.

If the ring still won't come loose, the problem may be corrosion, as explained in the next section.

REEL-SEAT CORROSION

Locking rings frozen due to corrosion or a reel seat that has been corroded by exposure to salt water can be treated in few different ways, provided that the corrosion is not too severe. A badly corroded reel seat, even if successfully cleaned up, may no longer be functional.

The most benign approach is to scrub the base of the stuck ring or the corroded part of the reel seat with lemon juice or vinegar, or let the reel seat soak for a while, and then scrub.

If you need to get more aggressive, use the methods explained in the section on "Rust and Corrosion," page 81. When using the commercial rust and corrosion removers noted in that section, mask off wood reel-seat inserts or rubber components with tape just to be safe. Use a small paintbrush to apply these compounds at the base of the locking ring or on corroded areas of the reel seat. Soak them only as a last resort.

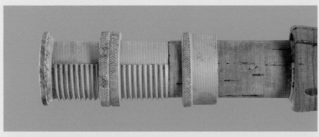

This reel seat shows light corrosion with some heavier pitting on the rings. The screw ring and threads stick and bind.

The seat and rings were first treated with Aluminum Jelly to remove the surface corrosion. The deeper pits were buffed out with a Dremel tool and wire wheel. It doesn't look quite like new, but it is perfectly functional.

If you succeed in freeing up frozen rings or removing corrosion to the point where the reel seat is usable again, you'll need to take precautions to prevent further deterioration. The etching and pitting that will be left in the metal are prime spots for new corrosion to take hold. Be conscientious about keeping a thin film of light oil over these areas.

If all these measures fail, and the locking rings are still stuck or corrosion has severely damaged the reel seat, you have little recourse but to replace the entire reel seat, as explained on page 50.

LOOSE-FITTING REEL

If your reel fits loosely on the rod—that is, the reel seat itself is firmly secured to the shaft, but the reel wobbles in the seat—there's an incompatibility between the size of the reel feet and metal hoods that capture them. The feet of that particular reel could be overly small, or the reel-seat hoods may have been deformed or enlarged by repeated tightening over the larger feet of a different reel.

There are a few approaches here. You can wrap electrician's tape around the feet of the reel until you've built up enough bulk so that the feet fit firmly beneath the hoods, though afterward, the reel may not fit on other rods. Or you can wrap a band of tape around the barrel of the reel seat until you've increased the diameter to the point where the reel fits snugly, though afterward, other reels may not fit on the rod. You can also use a piece of adhesive-backed foam weatherstripping cut to the size and shape of the reel foot. Attach the adhesive side to the reel foot, making a foam shim between the foot and the reel seat.

None of these is a particularly elegant solution, nor are any of them permanent. But they will fix the problem and are easy to redo when the tape or foam wears out.

LOOSE LOCKING RINGS

Sometimes the locking rings on a reel seat that secure the hood over the reel foot will persistently loosen during fishing. There is no permanent fix for this problem short of replacing the reel seat. But you can temporarily remedy the problem with the type of Teflon plumber's tape used to help waterproof pipe joints and plumbing fixtures. This is a nonadhesive tape, very thin and elastic, and there are two keys in applying it. First, wrap the tape very tightly around the threads on the reel seat; and second, wrap the tape in the same direction that the locking ring is tightened. If the tape is wrapped in the wrong direction, tightening the locking ring may cause the tape to peel off. Wrap a layer or two of tape; then test-fit the locking ring. If doesn't feel snug, add additional layers of tape. The tape may, or may not, stay on the threads when the locking ring is unscrewed; if it comes off, there's no other choice but to rewrap the threads next time you mount the reel.

LOOSE BUTT CAP

A butt cap that is loose or has come off can easily be reglued. If the cap is loose, work it free from the seat. Since the glue bond is already broken, it should come off without much trouble. Use a pocketknife to scrape away any dried glue from the contact surfaces, and then wipe them with rubbing alcohol. Test-fit the piece to make sure it slides easily back into position.

On uplocking reel seats—ones that screw up toward the rod tip—the butt cap is typically a button-type plug or metal cup at the end of the seat; you simply glue it on. On downlocking seats—ones that screw down toward the butt of the rod—the butt cap also functions as the hood that holds the reel foot, and two precautions are necessary here. First, wrap a strip of masking tape around the barrel of the reel seat. Sight down the rod, and mark a line on the masking tape that is in direct alignment with the guides on the butt section. When you reglue the butt cap, you want the hood to be centered on this line to ensure that the reel will be mounted on the rod in the proper position. Second, when applying the glue to the inside of the butt cap, don't get any adhesive under the hood itself. If you get a glob of dried glue beneath the hood the reel foot may not fit inside.

Spread waterproof epoxy or rod builder's glue on the contact surface of the butt cap and slide it into position. Use a rag dampened with alcohol to wipe away any excess glue before it dries.

LOOSE REEL SEAT

If the reel seat itself is loose and wiggles or turns on the rod shaft, the best way to effect a solid repair is to remove the reel seat and reglue it. Since the glue bond is broken, or partially broken, you may be able to remove the seat by twisting it and pulling the seat off the butt end of the rod. Take your time with this, working the seat back and forth as you pull. There are probably high spots of dried glue beneath the seat that you'll need to wear down or break off before the seat slides off. If the seat still won't pull free of the shaft, you can try the hot-water or heat-gun methods explained in "Removing a Reel Seat," page 45.

If applying heat fails to soften the glue enough to slip the seat off, you have two choices, neither of which, frankly, is very pretty. You can cut off the old reel seat as shown in "Removing a Reel Seat," which of course destroys it, and remount a new seat. Or you can try the following method. It does cosmetically mar the rod a bit, it's a little involved, and its success depends to some extent on how the original reel seat was mounted. But it works in many cases and is usually easier than replacing the entire seat.

This repair involves drilling a few holes in the barrel of the seat and injecting glue beneath the reel seat. Part of the trick here is finding the proper dispenser for the glue.

- Look at a hobby store or fly shop for a gel-type cyanoacrylate (CA) glue with a fine-tipped dispenser. Some brands, such as Zap, offer tubelike extender tips that work well. Make sure, however, that the glue is a gel type, not a liquid.
- Some hobby stores carry plastic syringes with long, tapering plastic tips or blunt metal tips; look for one that tapers down to about 1/16 inch in diameter. You can use this syringe to dispense epoxy or rod builder's glue. If you're using epoxy, make sure that you get a waterproof formula with a working time of at least an hour.

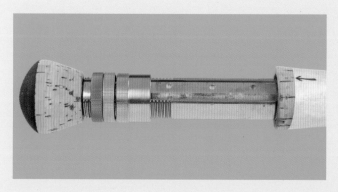

STEP 1: Wrap a strip of masking tape around the rear end of the cork grip. Mark the tape with a line that is in alignment with the guides on the butt section of the rod, as shown here. When you reglue the seat, you want to make sure that it's properly positioned so that the reel lines up with the guides on the rod.

In the barrel of the reel seat (not on the threaded portion), drill three or four evenly spaced holes that are slightly larger than the glue-dispenser tip. (The holes here are slightly larger than necessary for better visibility in the photo.) If you drill these on the underside of the barrel, as pictured above, they won't be visible when the reel is mounted.

How deep to drill depends on the way the reel seat has been mounted. If you consult the photo in Step 2, page 47, you'll see that the rod at the top of the picture had a reel seat mounted directly over the rod shaft itself. In this case, you want to drill right down to the shaft (but not through it) since the glue bond between the reel seat and the rod shaft has been broken.

Or, as shown on the rod at the bottom of the picture on page 47, the reel seat may have been mounted over a wooden or tape bushing. In this case, you'll have to determine where the glue bond has failed—between the reel seat and the bushing or between the bushing and the rod shaft. Drill just through the reel seat and barely into the bushing. Then turn the reel seat; if the bushing remains stationary, you know that the glue should be applied between the seat and the bushing, and you've drilled deep enough. If the bushing turns along with the reel seat, you know that the glue joint between the bushing and the shaft has failed, and you'll need to drill down to, but not through, the shaft and apply glue there.

STEP 2: If you're using a syringe, fill it with mixed epoxy or rod builder's glue. Insert the tip of the syringe or glue dispenser into one of the holes, and squirt in some glue. Hold the reel seat in position, with the holes facing upward. Rotate the shaft very slightly, and apply more glue. Keep rotating the shaft and applying glue until no more will go in. The idea here is to fill any voids or gaps beneath the seat, turning the rod to draw glue from the access hole and spread it around the shaft. Here, the hole at the left

is full and will accept no more adhesive when the reel seat is turned. When you've finished with one hole, move to the next, until you've put as much glue beneath the seat as possible.

When you're finished, turn the shaft until the underside of the reel seat is centered at the mark you made on the masking tape to align the seat the with the guides. Lay the rod down so that the holes face upward, and if necessary fill the holes with glue to be about flush with the barrel of the seat. Filling them will prevent any water from seeping under the reel seat.

REMOVING A REEL SEAT

If a loose reel seat can't be repaired by drilling and gluing, as explained above, or you don't wish to mar the appearance of the seat, you'll need to remove the seat and reglue it. And of course if a reel seat is damaged or corroded beyond use, you'll need to remove it and install a new one. Removing a reel seat can be more complicated, or less, depending on the type of reel seat and the adhesive originally used to mount it.

If the seat is mounted with a glue that softens or breaks down under heat (some epoxies are of this type), the hot-water method or the heat-gun method shown below may work. But if they don't, you must cut the old seat off the shaft; this takes patience, care, a steady hand, and a good attitude.

HOT-WATER METHOD. The hot-water method of removing the reel seat has the virtue of being the safest in the sense of posing virtually no risk to your rod since the reel seat never gets hotter than the temperature of boiling water. It can be used with reel seats of any material—aluminum, wood insert, graphite, plasticlike composites. However, it takes more time than the heat-gun method, and the relatively low temperature involved may not be sufficient to soften the glue. The heat-gun method is faster if you use a higher temperature setting, but these tools can produce very hot air—500 degrees or more—and without care and attention during use, they can scorch a cork grip or wood insert. But this approach is usually successful. Cutting away the reel seat is the brute-force approach; it takes the most time, is the most tedious, and runs the greatest risk of damaging the rod. But sometimes it's the only way.

Here's what you'll need for the hot-water method of removing the seat:
- A pan at least 6 inches deep and a heat source to boil water
- A large, heat-resistant plastic bag of the type suited to oven baking or microwaving
- A pair of gloves

STEP 1: Fill the pan with water deep enough to cover the reel seat when the seat is submerged and the rod held vertically. If you have an uplocking seat, use enough water to cover the lowermost cork ring as well, since you want to soften the glue holding the concealed ring beneath the cork. Heat the water to boiling, and turn it down to a simmer.

Insert the seat and grip into the plastic bag, and secure the bag opening around the rod shaft with a rubber band or twist-tie. Hold the rod vertically and immerse the reel seat in the simmering water. This process can take some time, and you can use a piece of coat hanger or uninsulated wire to fashion a bracket that holds the rod upright in the pot, so that you don't have to support it with your hands.

STEP 2: Leave the reel seat in the water for about 10 minutes. Then with gloved hands, grab the cork grip and reel seat (without removing the plastic bag), and twist in opposite directions. If the seat will not come off, put it back in the water.

Periodically check the seat to see if the seat has loosened. If not, return it to the water. When the glue finally begins to soften, you can twist and pull the old seat off.

If, after 30 minutes or so, the reel seat will not twist or loosen, further immersion is probably pointless, and you'll have to try the heat-gun method or cut the seat off.

But if you succeed, you'll see something like the rod at the top, which has a reel seat that was fitted directly over the shaft. Or you may see something like the rod on the bottom. The reel seat on this rod has an internal diameter much larger than the rod butt, so the shaft that was fitted with a wooden bushing, which is what you see here, to make the seat fit snugly. (On some rods, you may see bands of masking tape that serve the same purpose as the bushing.) Notice the butt of this lower rod where the seat was mounted; heat doesn't melt the glue, but rather breaks it down to a slightly sticky powder. It appears here as a whitish residue on the bushing. If the reel seat was simply loose and you removed it in order to reglue it, you can leave this bushing in place. Just clean it up as explained in "Installing a Reel Seat," Step 1, page 50.

Notice, too, that these are both uplocking reel seats. Heat transferred through the reel seat will loosen the glue that holds the hood that's concealed beneath the cork. The hood may slip off with the reel seat, as shown at the top. Or it may remain under the rearmost cork ring; if this is the case, just grab the hood carefully with needle-nose pliers and pull it out from under the cork.

HEAT-GUN METHOD. Heat guns are basically supercharged hair dryers, used for stripping paint, removing old floor tiles, and so on, and are usually available at tool rental outfits. Most have a variable temperature control and get quite hot at their maximum setting. This method is suitable for aluminum reel seats and those with wood inserts, though if your reel seat has a rubber button at the butt, remove it first to avoid melting it. A heat gun can be used on graphite or composite reel seats, but be prepared to replace the seat with a new one. The high heat may damage the original seat and make it unusable. In general, I find the approach described here to give very good results.

Here's what you need for the heat-gun method:

- Heat gun
- A heavy leather glove, like a fireplace glove; or an oven mitt

The process here goes pretty much as you'd think—heating up the reel seat and periodically checking to see if it's loose.

Step 1: Set the temperature control on the heat gun to a high setting. Direct the jet of hot air at the reel seat only. On an all-aluminum seat, you can put the nozzle of the heat gun very close to the metal, almost touching it, to speed up the heating process. On a seat with a wood insert, however, keep the nozzle a few inches from the reel seat and work more slowly. If you get the heat too close, it will scorch the wood.

Two cautions here: First, make sure that the hot-air stream is directed well away from your body and any flammable or combustible materials. Second, keep the reel seat moving, rotating it slowly in the hot air stream to prevent overheating one section or charring a wood insert or the cork.

Step 2: Heat the reel seat for a minute or two. With a gloved hand, twist and pull on the seat. If it doesn't move, continue heating for another minute or two and try again. If the seat doesn't loosen after you've heated for a total of 5 or 10 minutes, you'll probably have to cut it off. Note that reel seats with wood inserts will probably take more time than metal ones; wood is not a particularly good conductor and it takes longer for the heat to travel through the insert to the glue beneath.

If you're successful, you'll see something like that shown above in Step 2.

CUTTING OFF A REEL SEAT. This is a kind of ad-libbed affair, depending on the tools you have and the particular reel seat involved, and there is some risk of damaging the rod shaft even if you are careful. I consider it a last resort, but sometimes it's the only way. The process involves cutting through the reel seat, without touching the shaft beneath, and then prying the old seat off.

You can make the cut in a few different ways. Using a band saw, if you have access to one, is probably the fastest method and the one that gives you the most control. A Dremel-type tool with an abrasive cutoff wheel also works, though tools like this are a little more difficult to control precisely. If you take this approach, it's best to have another person hold the rod firmly against a bench or tabletop so that you can use both hands to steady and guide the tool. The slowest, but perhaps safest way, is to use a hacksaw with a very sharp blade. Again, having assistance in holding the rod helps.

STEP 1: First, cut or grind off any locking rings and sliding hoods; it will simplify removing the seat. (On the reel seat pictured here, it wasn't really necessary; the lower ring is already broken and the upper one so corroded that it will snap off easily.)

Then cut a slot down to, but not touching, the rod shaft. A cut that spirals down the reel seat, as shown here, has two advantages over a straight cut. It allows you to work around the seat to break the glue bond, and you can cut into the seat much closer to the rear of the cork grip than you could with a straight longitudinal cut.

STEP 2: After the cut is made, insert a flat, wide-bladed screwdriver into the slot and twist. Work up and down the slot in small increments. The idea here is to snap the glue bond so that the reel seat will slide off the end of the shaft.

In reality, though, there are any number of possible outcomes. A metal reel seat may tear. You can try to pull off strips or pieces of metal with a pair of vise grips, or you can grab a ragged edge of metal with a pair of needle-nose pliers, and roll the pliers, peeling part of the reel seat off. A wood insert may crack off in chunks or splinters. It's not always possible to tell what will happen, and you may need to exercise a little imagination to remove the seat.

On an uplocking seat, the upper hood may come off with the barrel of the reel seat or it may still remain concealed beneath the lowermost cork ring. If it doesn't come off, use needle-nose pliers to work it free. You can also try using a heat gun to loosen it first. Your top priority, however, is not damaging the cork; it's much easier to mount a new seat if this lowermost cork ring, which is bored out to accept the hood, remains intact.

Once the large pieces of the seat are split away from the rod shaft, use what tools you have—wood rasp, grinding wheel or hand grinder, sandpaper—to remove splinters of wood, dried glue, and so on.

INSTALLING A REEL SEAT

If you've removed a reel seat because it was loose, you can reglue the original seat provided it's in good condition. If you're installing a new reel seat, you will of course need the new seat itself.

You can attach the seat with waterproof epoxy or rod builder's glue. If using epoxy, choose one with a reasonably fast set-time; about 30 minutes is good. After the seat is glued, you want to apply some clamping pressure with your hands, and this can be tedious if the epoxy takes hours to set. Some rod builders favor polyurethane glues for their strength and waterproofness, but if you've never used this glue, you're probably better off avoiding it. Such glues foam up and expand to three or four times their original volume; it's easy to use too much. Glue seeps out of the joints, and it can be difficult to remove the excess.

Here's what you'll need to install the reel seat:
- New reel seat
- A roll of masking tape
- An electric drill with a bit larger than the butt diameter of the rod or a rat-tail file (only if the new reel seat won't fit over the rod butt)
- Waterproof epoxy or rod builder's glue
- Rubbing alcohol and a rag

STEP 1: To get a good glue bond, the rod shaft should be clean, as shown here. Scrape away any residue of old glue or any debris that adheres to the rod if you cut away the original seat. If the rod butt has a bushing on it, scrape, file, or sand away any residue for a clean surface; you want to get a surface that is round (so that the new reel seat will sit symmetrically on the shaft), and solid (for a good glue bond).

When glue site is prepared, wrap a strip of masking tape around the cork grip, and mark it with a line that is in alignment with the guides on the rod, as shown here. You'll need this reference mark when mounting the seat. It's an easy step to forget, and more than one rod builder has ended up with a seat that mounts the reel on top of the rod rather than underneath it.

Since the new reel seat is slipped over the butt of the rod, the hole through the seat must be larger in diameter than the rod butt. If the hole is too small, drill it out or use a rat-tail file to enlarge it. Make the hole big enough so that the seat slides over the shaft easily, and enlarge it symmetrically so that the seat is centered on the rod shaft.

STEP 2: Because the shaft is tapered and you may not get an exact fit of the reel seat to the shaft when you enlarge the hole, you'll need to shim the rod shaft so that the seat fits snugly. Wrap two or three evenly spaced bands of masking tape around the rod shaft so that the reel seat slides over the butt of the rod and fits without any looseness or wiggle. At the same time, the fit shouldn't be excessively tight or you may not get a solid glue joint. The seat should slip over the tape bands easily.

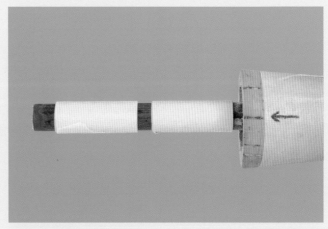

STEP 3: Now dry-fit the reel seat several times. One-piece reel seats of the type shown here are quite straightforward. But some uplocking seats, or some seats with wood inserts, or other specialty seats, have more than one piece, and you want to become thoroughly familiar with how these components fit together, what surfaces need gluing, and how all the pieces are aligned. Once you apply glue, you want to assemble the seat with confidence and a practiced hand.

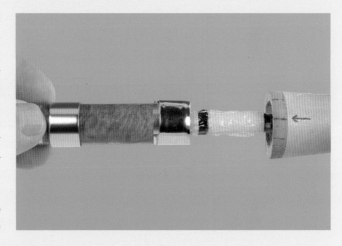

If the reel seat has multiple components, lay them out in the order in which they go on the rod shaft. For an uplocking seat with an insert, for instance, the order is: the upper hood and wood insert, barrel with threads, lower hood, locking ring(s), and butt cap.

Apply glue to the first component and mount. Continue applying glue to each component in its turn and then mounting it. When you come to mount the wood insert (or when you are mounting the simple one-piece seat pictured above), apply glue liberally around the base and top of each tape wrap, as shown here.

As you mount the seat or components such as the hoods or an insert with a milled slot for the reel foot, check that each of these aligned with the mark on the masking tape that indicates the guide alignment.

STEP 4: When the entire seat is mounted, check the alignment of all components again, and make any necessary adjustments.

Then check carefully around the seat for any glue that may have seeped from underneath. Pay particular attention to the threads on the reel seat. Dried glue here could prevent

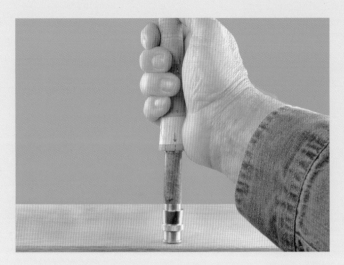

the locking rings from tightening or even glue them to the threads. Clean up any excess glue with a rag and alcohol.

Then hold the rod vertically, set the butt on the floor or tabletop, and press firmly downward to seat the components together. You don't need a lot of pressure, just enough for firm contact between the gluing surfaces. Hold it for a few minutes, periodically checking for any additional glue seepage and cleaning up an excess as needed.

REPAIRING A GRIP

Small gouges, tears, or chips in a cork grip can easily be repaired by filling them with a putty made of sanded cork dust and glue. Indeed, this is how pits and other imperfections in the cork are often treated by the manufacturer to improve the appearance of the grip.

The only real stipulation for the glue is that it be waterproof. I've had good results with waterproof carpenter's or woodworker's glue; it dries clear, at least more or less, and sands down fairly easily. Epoxies can be tough to sand down, and glues that dry to a dark color don't blend well with the color of the cork.

For the cork dust, use a cork ring sold for rod grips. Wine corks and other such sources can be contaminated.

Here's what you'll need:
- Sharp knife
- Cork ring
- Glue
- Aluminum foil
- Toothpick
- Popsicle-type sticks
- 100- and 220-grit sandpaper

STEP 1: For good adhesion, the gluing surface should be clean. You can wash the damaged area by using one of the methods explained on page 10 for cleaning a cork grip, but the let the cork dry thoroughly. Or you can use the point of a sharp knife to cut or scrape away the dirty surfaces of the gouge or nick or remove any crumbling cork, as shown here. You want a clean, solid patching surface for good glue adhesion.

With 100-grit sandpaper, sand the cork ring to produce enough sawdust to fill the damaged area, as shown at the left. On a piece of aluminum foil, use a toothpick to mix the sawdust with a small amount of glue. Add more glue as needed to get a paste about the consistency of wood filler putty, as shown at the right.

STEP 2: Spread the putty into the damaged area. Pack it in firmly, and smooth the patch to blend with the surrounding cork, but leave a low mound of excess putty over the repair. The surface of the patch should stand a little higher than the surface of the grip. Sanding this excess away will produce a smooth, nicely blended repair.

STEP 3: When the putty dries, use sandpaper to remove the excess dried filler, working to smooth the patch to the contour of the grip. A small sanding block can help prevent removing material from the intact portion of the grip as you work on the patch. If there's a lot of excess putty or a large repair area, start with 100-grit sandpaper for faster cutting. When the patch is nearly to its final dimensions,

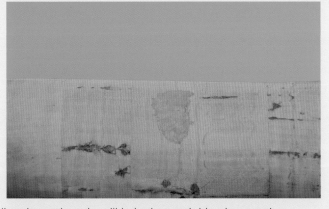

switch to 220 grit. Finally, lightly sanding the entire grip will help the patch blend cosmetically with the rest of the cork.

The putty method works well for most repairs, though for deeper gouges, you may need to apply the putty in stages, letting each layer dry before applying the next. Occasionally, however, a piece of cork is torn from the front or rear edge of the grip, particularly in flared grip designs such as the various Wells-style grips. You can in fact fix these with putty, but a cork patch is more aesthetically pleasing and may prove more durable if the damage has occurred in a high-wear area such as the part of the grip that lies beneath your thumb. The aim here is simply to cut away the damaged area and glue in a separate patch of cork.

To make a cork patch, you'll need:
- Cork ring
- A very sharp knife or single-edged razor blade
- Waterproof glue
- A small disposable paintbrush
- 150- and 220-grit sandpaper

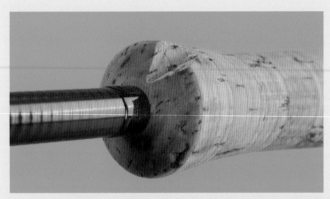

STEP 1: Cut away the damaged area with a very sharp blade; cork is soft, and a dull edge will mash or tear rather than slice. You want to trim the cork in a shape that will be easy to fit with the patch. Cutting a simple wedge shape, as shown here, works well. It can be done in two straight, clean strokes, and the resulting geometry is reasonably easy to match when you cut the patch.

If the damage has occurred at the front or rear edge of the grip, you may want to wrap the portion of the rod shaft or reel seat next to the grip in several layers of masking tape to protect it when you're cutting, gluing, and sanding.

STEP 2: From a cork ring, cut a patch. Take your best guess at a matching shape; then test-fit the patch and trim as needed. For the best appearance, get the closest match you can between the patch and the cut; the tighter the fit, the better it will look. As shown here, leave the patch oversize. You'll bring it to final shape with sandpaper.

When the patch fits, use the paintbrush to spread a thin film of the glue into the cut. Insert the patch. If you wish, you can wrap a band of masking tape around the patch, completely encircling the grip to the clamp the cork in position. Or you can use straight pins to pin the patch in place.

STEP 3: When the glue dries, sand the patch to match the contours of the grip. If there are any gaps in the seam of the patch, you can use the putty method described above to fill them. Sand down any putty, and give a light sanding to the entire grip for a uniform color.

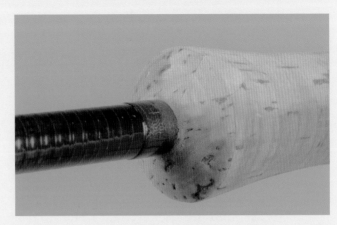

FIELD FIXES

Emergency repairs in the field are usually temporary and never particularly elegant or attractive. But they can keep a rod in fishable condition for the duration of a trip; when you return home, you can undertake a more permanent fix. The repairs explained here assume that you are supplied with at least some of the basic materials listed in "Field Kit," Chapter 6.

ROD SHAFT

A rod shaft that's been nicked or chipped deeply enough to present a potential weak spot can be reinforced, though as always in this type of repair, success depends upon the severity of the damage.

Clean the shaft surrounding the damaged area as best you can. Cut an 8-inch strip of fiberglass-reinforced packing tape about ½ to ¾ inch wide. Beginning about an inch beyond the damage, wrap the tape very tightly around the shaft. Spiral the tape over the damaged area in slightly overlapping turns, finishing about an inch beyond the damage. Cut off the excess tape. Wrapping tip sections tightly can be tricky since they will flex under heavy pressure. It can go a little more easily if you split the tape lengthwise first to make a narrower strip, which allows you to support the shaft closer to the wrapping point.

Use thread to overwrap the tape tightly, as shown in the procedure on pages 18–21, forming a continuous band of thread that extends slightly beyond both ends of the tape. (In a pinch, you can use 3X or 4X tippet material if you have no thread, but fluorocarbon is better than nylon mono since it has less stretch.) It's quite possible that you won't have a cardboard box, a book, and the other materials for a rod-wrapping setup, and you'll have to improvise a bit. Have a partner pinch the spool of thread to apply tension as you hold and wrap the rod section. Or cup the spool of thread in your hand and wrap tightly over the damaged area, feeding thread as you need it.

When the wrap is complete, cover both ends of the wrapping with a band of tape to prevent the thread from unraveling.

TIP-TOP AND BROKEN TIP

A tip-top that is loose or has come off can be remounted as shown on page 36. Ferrule cement is best, but almost any type of adhesive will do, including the Aquaseal you may have packed for wader repair, though this takes awhile to dry.

You may be able to salvage a broken rod tip by mounting a new tip-top using the method explained on page 36, and again you'll need to cut away any damaged or split portion of the shaft to mount the tip-top on a sound portion of the rod. You can use the file, or even nail file, on a multitool, or the edge of a ceramic or diamond hook hone to work around the shaft, as shown in that procedure, to score the tip deeply enough to snap it off.

If you lack a properly sized tip-top, trim the rod shaft off directly above the first intact snake guide, which will then function as the tip-top. But don't leave too much excess rod shaft beyond the guide or the line can wrap around it during fishing.

LOOSE FERRULE

There are a couple of quick fixes to a ferrule that is so loose it separates during fishing. If the ferrule is obviously worn, try applying a little candle wax to the ferrule; the lubrication may help seat the male end more deeply. Or you can shim the male end by covering it with a piece of plastic sandwich wrap or plastic bag before joining the rod sections. Then tear away the excess plastic.

As noted earlier, a loose ferrule is often symptomatic of a cracked female end, and fishing the rod or shimming the ferrule can make the problem worse. If you're in doubt about the structural integrity of the ferrule, you may want to perform the following repair.

CRACKED FERRULE

If there's a visible crack in the ferrule or the quick fixes above give no result, you can reinforce the ferrule area by overwrapping it just as you would a damaged rod shaft. Clean the female ferrule. Cut a strip of fiberglass-reinforced packing tape ½ to ¾ inch wide, and very tightly wrap the entire ferrule. If there is a snake guide mounted on the ferrule, you'll have to make these wraps in two stages, one on each side of the guide. Begin the wrap as close as you can get to the lip of the ferrule, and extend it about an inch beyond the upper end of the ferrule. Then tightly overwrap the tape with thread or tippet material, again with fluorocarbon the better choice. Since the ferrule is at the end of the rod section, it's a fairly easy matter to hold a spool of thread or tippet material in your palm as you make these wraps; a box stand or support isn't really necessary. When you're finished, wrap a band of tape around each end of the thread wrap to prevent it from unraveling.

Loose Guide

A loose guide may pose little problem in your fishing, but it is worth attending to since the guide foot shifting around under the wraps could damage the rod shaft. You may be able to secure a loose guide with a bit of adhesive applied under the guide itself at the end of the thread wraps, in the small void between the guide foot and the rod shaft. If you have ferrule cement, try it first; should you decide to rewrap the guide at some point, this is the easiest adhesive to remove. Clean the contact areas as best you can, and apply the cement liberally. You may need to sharpen the stick of cement to a point, or shave off a tapered sliver to get the adhesive into that fairly restricted space. Gel-type cyanoacrylate glue can also be used, though it will be more difficult to remove later. If you don't wish to use glue, you may have success by wrapping thread, tippet material, or a thin strip of packing tape around the bare portion of the guide between the thread wraps and the frame. Wrap it firmly and, if using thread or tippet, cover the wrap with tape. Test to see if the guide is still loose; the wrapping area is narrow, and you may or may not get enough rigidity to immobilize the guide.

An excessively loose guide that moves freely beneath the thread wraps, or one in danger of coming off, may need to be remounted. This is not as extreme as it sounds. With a sharp knife or razor blade held flat atop the guide foot, slice down the top of the foot, cutting away the strip of varnish and thread wraps covering the foot. When both feet are exposed, lift the guide free. If you can peel off any of the thread wraps and varnish, that's fine, but not necessary. If the varnish is intact, you'll need to shave down the ridges of thread and varnish left by the sides of the guide foot. This will expose enough contact area on the top of the guide foot so that the new thread wraps will bind it to the shaft. Working parallel to the shank, carefully shave down these ridges. Don't try to remove them completely; you might nick the shaft.

Rewrap the guide as explained on page 30, using any kind of thread or light tippet material. Wrap firmly but not tightly; it doesn't take a great deal of tension to hold a guide in place. Again, having a partner hold the thread spool is probably the easiest approach here for getting tension on the thread. If you're working alone, a cut length of thread—say, 24 inches—is easier to work with than a spool and sufficiently long to wrap most fly-rod guides. Then cover the thread wraps with a strip of tape to prevent them from unraveling.

A quicker, but potentially less durable, version of this repair uses a thin strip of packing tape instead of thread. (Duct or electrician's tape may be too elastic to hold the guide firmly.) But you may find that water loosens the tape adhesive after a time.

LOOSE REEL SEAT OR BUTT CAP

A reel seat that continually loosens or a reel that does not fit tightly can be secured as explained on page 43, by wrapping the feet of the reel or the barrel of the reel seat with tape to give a tight fit. If the problem is extreme, you can simply wrap the entire reel seat, essentially taping the reel to the rod. It's actually surprising how well this holds. Electrician's tape is a good choice because it is fairly water resistant.

The best fix for a loose butt cap is regluing if you have a suitable adhesive, since this is a pretty simple job. Even ferrule cement will hold for a time and is easy to remove for a more permanent repair. In the absence of glue, your best bet is to hold the cap in place with duct or electrician's tape. Take a "strap" of tape around the back of the butt cap and secure the ends to the seat; then take additional wraps of tape around the butt end of the reel seat, securing the ends of the strap. Chances are, especially on a downlocking seat, that the tape wraps will interfere with mounting the reel, and you may need to secure the butt cap with the reel affixed to the rod.

BAMBOO RODS

A quality bamboo rod is not only a delightful fishing instrument, but a pride-of-ownership piece of equipment and well worth the bit of extra care it requires. A well-maintained cane rod will give long service and hold its value over the years. Virtually all the points made earlier in this chapter about the precautions, care, and maintenance surrounding rods made of synthetic materials hold for bamboo rods as well, though, as explained below, there are some differences and a few points so important that they bear repeating.

PRECAUTIONS
- Assembling and disassembling a cane rod differs from the procedure used with graphite and fiberglass rods. To assemble the rod, grasp one section at the base of the male ferrule; hold the other section 6 to 12 inches above the female

ferrule. Mate the ferrules until they just touch, align the guides, and push the rod sections straight together. To break down the rod, reverse the procedure, again pulling the rod sections straight apart. Never twist or flex the sections of a bamboo rod when you are joining or taking them apart. Metal ferrules are strong but they are not designed or installed to withstand torque. A rod-repair person told me that one of the more common types of damage he sees is a cane rod section broken at the base of the female ferrule—often attributable to bending and twisting the shaft during disassembly.

To separate particularly stubborn ferrules, the two-man method shown on page 6 is recommended as the safest for the rod.

- A great many bamboo rods are made with two matching tips, and most rod-makers recommend the tips be used alternately, tip 1 on one day, tip 2 on the second, tip 1 on the third, and so on. You can use a small plastic twist-tie secured to the tip-top of the rod tip that is to be used on the next trip, switching it back and forth between the tips to keep track of the sequence.

- Extra attention is required to protect bamboo rods from excessive heat. As explained earlier, even graphite rods that are subjected to high heat when flexed can acquire a permanent bend. This is doubly true of cane rods. In fact, during the construction of a cane rod, the sections of bamboo are straightened by a careful application of heat and strategic bending; the shaft can easily be unstraightened by careless exposure to heat and bending, such as leaving a flexed rod in a closed car or trunk on a sunny day. The rod, particularly the tip, can take a "set"; that is, the shaft will remain bent at the point of flex. Though set can be removed from a cane rod, straightening a shaft is a job best left to professional hands.

- Some rod finishes are very susceptible to breakdown by heat. Avoid laying a rod or rod sections on the hood or top of a car in hot weather. If you've ever leaned against a car that's been sitting in the sun all day, you know how surprisingly hot the metal can get. If part of the rod shaft contacts this hot surface, it could be damaged.

- By nature, bamboo is considerably more malleable than graphite or fiberglass, and a rod can take a set if the shaft is left in a flexed position for a prolonged time, even at normal temperatures. The safest course is to make sure that the rod or sections are fully relaxed, under no tension, when the rod is not being fished. Never, for instance, leave an assembled rod leaning against a wall for an extended period of time; a light trout rod may acquire a set in a matter of weeks.

- Take particular care to protect a cane rod shaft from contact with solvents or insect repellents containing DEET. The varnish used to finish many bamboo rods is highly vulnerable to chemicals of this kind and can be softened or eaten away.

● Though bamboo rods are quite strong, a little conscientiousness and common sense in fishing will help keep them in top condition. Many rodmakers recommend that, when playing fish, you periodically rotate your rod hand 180 degrees, so that the reel faces upward, to vary the direction of flex in the rod and equalize the stresses on the shaft. It will minimize the possibility of the rod taking a set from constant bending in one direction.

   If you snag up when fishing, don't reef on a cane rod in hopes of pulling the fly free. The rod can easily be overstressed. Instead, strip out some slack; grab the line beyond the rod tip and pull hand-over-hand to free the fly or break it off.

   By the same token, don't habitually pursue large fish on light bamboo tackle. Even more than with graphite or fiberglass rods, you should match the strength of a cane rod to the size of the fish.

   Pressure large fish more with the reel than with the rod; use a shallow rod angle and let fish fight against the drag tension.

● When you're done fishing for the day, break down and case your rod, and store it as explained below. If a cane rod is left assembled for long periods, the metal ferrules can oxidize and freeze up. Separating the sections without damaging the rod or ferrules often requires a repair expert.

● When casing (and uncasing) a bamboo rod, it's wise to cup your hand around the mouth of the rod tube, using your fingers to form a ring smaller in diameter than the tube itself. Then pull the rod bag out of the tube. Your fingers form a bumper that prevents that rod and the guides from scraping against the metal mouth of the tube. Never reach into the tube and pull rod sections directly from the bag; should they rub the metal tube, the finish may be damaged.

CARE AND MAINTENANCE

Maintaining a cane rod is in some respects no different from caring for a graphite or fiberglass one, but because the shaft is constructed of a natural material and the ferrule is metal rather than a relatively inert composite, there are some differences worth heeding.

CLEANING. All bamboo rod shafts can be cleaned simply by wiping them down with a damp cloth and drying them thoroughly. Because the beauty of cane is one of the pleasures in owning and fishing it, many anglers choose to polish the rod after cleaning to maintain its appearance. A good-quality furniture polish does an excellent job, though some rodmakers caution against using any products containing silicone.

Apply the polish sparingly, and buff the shaft to a luster with a soft, clean cloth. One rod-repair expert, however, offered this piece of advice. When polishing, begin softly and slowly. If a cane rod begins to fracture, particularly in the thin tip section, the separation of the material may begin as a small sliver splitting off from the shaft. If you work carefully and lightly, you may be able to detect this sliver as the weave of the rag snags momentarily on the splinter edge. But if you polish too aggressively, the rag may catch and hold the sliver, and under the force of rubbing, it may raise this splinter of material, drag it down the shaft, and enlarge the damage. Should you discover a splinter of this sort, flag the spot immediately, and under no circumstances fish the rod.

One of the inflexible rules in caring for a cane rod is to keep the ferrules clean. The ferrule material is typically nickel silver, sometimes called "German silver," though it in fact contains no silver at all but is an alloy of copper, nickel, and zinc. This alloy is relatively soft as metals go, and any dirt, grit, or abrasive material trapped in a mated ferrule will wear away the surfaces and produce a ferrule that will no longer fit tightly or exhibits some internal play during casting, which in turn accelerates the wear even more.

Various cleaning techniques are used. Some rodmakers advise wiping down the male ferrule with a soft cloth and denatured alcohol, then using a cotton swab damp with alcohol to clean the inside of the female ferrule. This method is effective in removing oily residue, but you must be extremely careful not to allow any alcohol to come into contact with the rod shaft or thread wraps as it can attack some types of varnish.

Ron White, a cane rodmaker at Orvis for 37 years, takes a different approach. He smears a small dab—don't overdo it—of Vaseline petroleum jelly on the male ferrule, then slides it in and out of the mating ferrule. Note that this is not for the purpose of lubrication, of which more in a moment; rather, the Vaseline loosens any dirt trapped in the female ferrule. Then he thoroughly cleans off the Vaseline, wiping down the male ferrule and using a cotton swab to remove all residue from the female end.

Regardless of the technique used, however, clean ferrules are vital to keeping the rod trouble-free. It is a small task to wipe down the ferrules each time you assemble a rod and again when you disassemble and dry the sections after fishing.

Occasionally, metal ferrules—even on a rod that has been stored properly—will oxidize to the point that mating them can be a problem. Good ferrule fit relies on a clean, smoothly polished surface; heavy oxidation is slightly rough and can produce enough friction and resistance to prevent the ferrule from seating properly. Don't use brute force to join ferrules in this condition; you could damage the rod. And if you succeed in joining the sections, you may not be able to get them apart later. The oxidation needs to be removed before the rod can be assembled and used.

I spoke with a number of cane rodmakers about the problem, and though they differed some in their recommendations, they were unanimous on one point: Don't resort to heavy abrasives—sandpaper, emery cloth, even harsh rubbing compounds—to remove oxidation. As noted earlier, ferrule material is relatively soft, and even mild abrasives in overzealous hands can change a ferrule's dimensions to the point that it no longer fits tightly. Instead, one rodmaker advised using a jeweler's cloth, a treated fabric used to restore luster to precious metals. Wipe down the male ferrule repeatedly until no more residue is removed. Use a cotton swab to push a strip of the cloth inside the female ferrule to clean it. A second rodmaker advised using 0000 steel wool, rubbing with very light pressure. Other sources suggested a high-quality, soft, nonscratching paste polish such as Simichrome or Noxon, following the directions on the container and making sure to completely remove any polish residue. But in all cases, work slowly and gently, checking the ferrule fit frequently. Liquid chemical cleaners and "dip" polishes such as Tarnex are not recommended. They can leave residues on the ferrule that are very difficult to remove, and some of these compounds can actually etch the metal.

As far as cleaning grips and reel seats, the methods described earlier in this chapter are suitable for cane rods as well. But anytime abrasives are used—in sanding a dirty grip, for example—it is worth taking extra precautions to mask off and protect the rod shaft itself from accidental scratching.

LUBRICATING FERRULES. In a word—don't. Lubricants trap dirt, grit, and abrasive particles that cause wear on the ferrules. The time-honored method of rubbing a male ferrule alongside your nose to lubricate the metal with oil from your skin is particularly heinous. Not only will the ferrule pick up contaminants, but the oil from your skin can be mildly corrosive to the metal, particularly if the ferrule is left assembled for an extended time. A squeaky-clean, dry, metal-to-metal contact promotes ferrule life.

STORAGE. Aside from avoiding accidental breakage, probably the most important measure you can take to ensure the long life of a cane rod is to protect it from the damaging effects of moisture—both water and damp air—by storing the rod properly. Moisture that penetrates a rod can soften the finish, weaken the rod fibers, compromise the glue joints, and damage the guide wrappings—and that's apart from the kind of corrosion and mildew that can afflict any type of rod, regardless of the material, that is put away wet.

After you are finished fishing for the day, dry the rod sections with a soft cloth, removing as much surface moisture as you can. Bag the sections and case them. When you return home, remove the bag from the tube and hang it up for a few hours to let the residual moisture evaporate. If the bag has become wet or damp from rain or humidity, remove the rod sections and air-dry the rod and bag separately. Leave the cap off the rod tube to let any moisture escape.

When everything is dry, bag and case the rod, and store the tube (vertically, according to rodmakers I spoke with) in an area not subject to extremes of heat or cold or to high humidity; anywhere indoors at room temperature is fine. One repair person I spoke with suggested putting a desiccant gel pack inside the rod tube for extra insurance against moisture. Under no circumstances should you leave a cane rod, cased or otherwise, in a damp basement or garage, or a very hot or very cold attic.

CHECKUP

Inspecting a cane rod to assess its condition is in some respects like examining any rod. You want to make sure that there is no corrosion on any of the metal components; that the tip-top is solidly mounted and aligned with the guides; that the guides themselves are tightly mounted; that the thread wraps are not frayed and the finish on the rod wrappings is intact; that the grip and reel seat are in good condition. Make a note of problems or potential problems that need attention, just as you would with any rod.

There are a couple of important differences with cane rods, however, and the first, of course, is the bamboo shaft, or more particularly the way the shaft is finished. Any discussion of bamboo rods quickly grows a little complicated, primarily because the rods in use today represent a number of different individual rodmakers, both past and present. These craftsmen used various adhesives and finishes on their rods, and indeed, even a single rodmaker may, over the course of his career, have used different glues and varnishes at different times. So generalizations about cane rods are just that—general.

There is, however, one useful distinction that can be drawn. Some cane rods are given a topical finish, usually a type of varnish, applied over the surface of the cane. Others, however, are impregnated, infused with a compound that renders the cane itself virtually waterproof and yields a fairly hard, tough exterior surface. If you are unsure about which type of rod you have, contact the maker or consult an experienced repair person or other individual qualified to make the determination, as the two types of shafts are evaluated a little differently when you inspect them.

With either type of shaft, however, check carefully for any scratches, nicks, chips, dings, and dents. As explained earlier, judicious polishing with a soft cloth may alert you to an area where the rod is beginning to splinter. Mark or make note of any damage.

If the rod is impregnated, you are pretty much done with the inspection after you've examined the shaft for any physical damage to the bamboo material itself. With a rod that is varnished, however, you should also assess the condition of the finish. On these types of rods, the varnish is more than simply cosmetic; it forms a waterproof barrier between the bamboo shaft and the outside world. This barrier is particularly important on older rods, assembled at a time when modern waterproof glues were unavailable; the adhesives used in older rods can lose their grip after being exposed to moisture for a time. If the finish is compromised, the glue seams can open and the rod can literally begin to come apart.

When evaluating the finish, look for any areas in which the varnish is cracked, chipped, crazed, blistered, or scratched through to the cane itself. These breaches in the protective finish can admit water into the shaft, so again, mark or make note of them.

The second big difference between bamboo and synthetic rods lies in the ferrules. Metal ferrules rarely crack in the way graphite or fiberglass ones will, but the fit can become loose as the ferrule wears. This looseness may be impossible to detect simply by hand-fitting the ferrule and checking for tightness. It may seem perfectly snug, when in reality the tip of the male ferrule may be worn enough to "wobble" inside the female ferrule. The only real clue you may have is in casting the rod, when you feel (or if the wear is extreme, even hear) a slight click or tick during each stroke of the cast as the end of the male ferrule rocks back and forth, tapping the interior walls of the female ferrule. In this case, a ferrule replacement is probably in your future.

Finally, check to see that the ferrules are firmly attached to the rod shaft. Pull straight outward on the ferrule (but don't twist it) to see if you can detect any play, and check for any cracking on the thread wraps at the base of the ferrules that might indicate that the ferrule is shifting around beneath the wrappings. A rod in this condition shouldn't be fished until the ferrules are reset.

What to do about any of the problems you may discover and note down is a point addressed in the next section.

REPAIR

The plain truth of the matter is this: If your cane rod is valuable, or you wish it to hold its value, or you intend to preserve it as a piece of heirloom equipment, you are substantially better off having any necessary repairs performed by a professional. One highly respected broker of collectible fly tackle once lamented to me how many fine rods had been diminished or even destroyed at the hands of well-meaning do-it-yourselfers. But even if your rod has more value as a personal fishing tool than as a collector's item, a professional repair very often makes sense when compared with the time and trouble of attempting it yourself and, often, with the quality of the finished job. Bamboo repair can be painstaking and exacting. Some tasks—straightening a section to remove the set, refinishing the shaft, mending a splintered-out shaft section, replacing or resetting ferrules, splicing a break—require experience, skill, and the proper supplies. However, if you wish to repair your own cane rods, there is a substantial amount of information in both electronic and print forms to set you on your way. But most cane-repair procedures are too specialized to fall within the scope of this book.

Having said that, there are a few simple repairs that you might wish to perform—not necessarily in lieu of a professional job, but as temporary measures that will allow you to fish the rod until a more permanent repair or restoration can be undertaken by an expert. These repairs—most of which are identical to the techniques used on synthetic rods—are summarized below; these are in a sense reversible. That is, they will put the rod in fishable condition, but undoing them won't prove an obstacle or permanently affect the rod when the time for a professional repair comes.

REWRAPPING OR REPLACING A GUIDE. It is no great matter to rewrap a loose guide, replace a guide that is damaged, or rewrap any thread wraps on a cane rod that are frayed or broken. The basic procedure is shown on page 37. But there are two important differences.

First is removing the old thread wraps and/or guide. The "solvent" technique shown on page 26 is highly ill advised for bamboo rods. At the very least, it will probably destroy the finish on the shaft; at worst, it could soften the glue holding the bamboo strips together. Fortunately, few, if any, cane rodmakers use the kind of high-build, two-part, one-step finish shown in that demonstration—precisely the kind of finish that is difficult to remove cleanly without solvents. Instead, they tend to use thinner, traditional varnishes with a lower build, and wraps coated with such a finish are much easier to remove; no chemicals are required. Simply use a razor blade to shave off the thread that lies atop the guide foot, and the remainder of the wrapping usually peels away with little trouble.

The second difference lies in finishing the thread wraps—don't use the kind of high-build, two-part finish noted above. Should you wish to have the job professionally done at a later date, the repair person may have great difficulty removing the old thread-wrap varnish. Instead, use spar varnish or, as one repair person suggested, even fingernail polish; it may take more than one coat, but both of these finishes can be easily removed when the time comes.

FINISH TOUCH-UPS. Light scratches or surface marring on an impregnated cane shaft are largely cosmetic and can usually be removed using 0000 steel wool, provided they are not too deep. After using the steel wool, polish and buff the shaft.

Damage to the finish of a varnished rod, however, can be more than a matter of aesthetics; the bamboo is exposed to water wherever the finish is compromised. Fortunately, nicks, chips, and scratches can be taken care of fairly easily. Use a fine-tipped brush to apply a thin coat of a high-quality spar varnish to the damaged area. When it is dry to the touch, apply a second thin coat if necessary, and then let the repair dry thoroughly, which can take several days. Cosmetically, it may not be perfect, but it will help prevent further cracking or chipping of the finish and protect the shaft from moisture damage. Should you ever choose to have the rod professionally refinished, your patch job won't cause any problems.

TIP-TOP. A tip-top that is loose or has come off the rod can be remounted using exactly the procedure shown on pages 36–38. However, if you plan to replace the tip-top on a rod section that's been broken, as shown on pages 38–40, you should consider consulting a professional first. Depending on the particular rod and the location of the break, an actual repair of the tip section might be possible.

CORK DAMAGE. Damage to a cork grip on a cane rod can be repaired using the methods beginning on page 52, though as already noted, take extra precautions to protect the rod shaft from any tools or abrasives that you might employ in the repair.

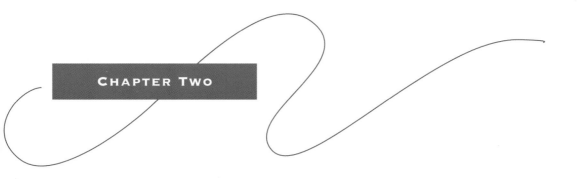

REELS

BECAUSE REELS ARE CONSTRUCTED primarily of metal components, they are in some respects more rugged than rods. The kinds of nicks, scratches, and dings that can seriously damage a rod are often inconsequential in a reel, amounting to little more than marred aesthetics—or honorable battle scars, depending on how you look at them. Unlike rods, where the chief cause of failure or breakage is an accident, reels are apt to suffer damage through neglect. Their mechanical simplicity and durable materials can mislead an angler into thinking that reels don't require much attention. And for the most part, they don't. But the downside of the relative toughness of reels is that mishap or neglect severe enough to inflict damage may be beyond the remedies of home repair. Taking precautions to protect a reel is the wisest course.

PREVENTION

- A severe impact can put a reel out of commission, bending the frame, spool, or handle. But even apparently superficial scratches or nicks that don't affect the mechanical operation of the reel may present potential problems. A scratch, for instance, deep enough to penetrate the anodized or powder-coated finish and expose bare metal underneath can offer an entry point for corrosion, particularly in saltwater reels.

    Unsurprisingly, the best way to protect the reel from impact and surface abrasion is to keep it cased when you're not fishing—especially during transport. A reel that's banging around in the back of a car or rattling against the bottom of a moving boat is a prime candidate for damage. Fortunately, most reel cases these days are designed with a flap-type top that will fasten over a reel seat so that the reel can be cased even when it's mounted on a rod and the rod is strung. In salt water, a case of this type also protects a reel against spray that can force seawater into the mechanical components.

- As with rods, don't subject a reel to excessive heat—leaving it in direct sunlight in a closed car, for instance—particularly when there is pressure on the drag disk or mechanism.

- When stringing up a rod, avoid setting the reel on the ground where it can pick up particles of dirt or sand that may find their way to the inside of the reel. If nothing else, put your hat on the ground upside down and set the reel inside while you're rigging the rod. If you happen to drop the reel in dirt or mud while you're fishing, give it a brief, soft swish in the water to rinse off the grit and prevent it from working its way to the interior.

- At the same time, however, don't submerge a reel or let it sit in boat bilge or standing water for more than a few moments. Material suspended in the water may contaminate drag surfaces or mechanical components, and even clean water can reduce drag friction to the point where some drags will hydroplane. And the longer a reel is submerged, the greater the likelihood that water will penetrate the drag mechanism, bearings, or other components and increase the risk of corrosion. If you do submerge the reel, shake it briskly to flush out any water that has made its way between the spool and frame.

- As with rods, keep a reel away from solvents, such as gasoline for boat engines. Though most components of the reel won't be affected, some drag materials could be damaged and the lubrication on drag surfaces or metal-to-metal contact points could be dissolved.

- When fishing, use a reel that is appropriate to the job—a particular caution these days when pursuing oversize fish with undersize tackle and other such feats of showmanship seem to be enjoying a certain vogue. Fishing 10-pound tippet on a light trout reel and cranking down the drag on a 15-pound coho subjects the reel to stresses for which it wasn't designed. The mere fact that the drag on a light reel can be tightened down to tarpon-stopping pressures doesn't automatically make doing so a good idea.

- By the same token, avoid—or at least be very cautious about—using freshwater reels in salt or brackish water. The materials used in a freshwater reel are not necessarily chosen with the corrosive effects of salt water in mind.

- When you're finished fishing—for the day or for the season—back the drag off to its lightest setting to take pressure off the drag components.

- Don't attempt to disassemble a factory-sealed drag. You may compromise its watertightness or void the warranty. Along the same lines, if some reel components are assembled with special fasteners—square- or star-head screws, for instance—it's best to leave them alone. Reel makers will intentionally use these unconventional parts precisely to discourage disassembly.

● Finally, when storing a reel, as with all gear, make sure it is completely dry. Store the reel uncased, or in a partially open case, to promote air circulation. A cased reel should be kept in a place with relatively stable temperature and humidity to prevent condensation from forming. And the case itself should be dry. If you've kept a saltwater reel cased when traveling in a boat, or if you put a wet reel into the case, you should wash the case to remove any salt or mineral residue that may come into contact with the reel.

CARE AND MAINTENANCE

Except for the angler, the reel is the only part of a fully equipped, onstream fly fisher that has actual moving parts. And as with most mechanical systems, contamination, corrosion, and lubrication are the primary concerns.

CLEANING

A reel should be washed to keep it clean; how and how often depends upon the conditions of use. A freshwater reel may need cleaning only once a season, though if it is used in excessively turbid or dirty water, it may need more frequent attention. If the reel has been dropped in the dirt, mud, or sand, it should be cleaned as soon as possible.

Cleaning a freshwater reel is a simple procedure that, in most cases, amounts to little more than rinsing off any contaminants. To wash the reel, remove the spool. If it has a disk drag or other adjustable drag, consult the manufacturer's instructions about cleaning. Some reel makers recommend rinsing a reel with the drag tightened down moderately to avoid loosened particles of dirt from being deposited onto the drag surfaces. In most cases, though, loosening the drag to its lightest setting will allow the water to flush any grit out of the drag mechanism. Rinse the reel frame inside and out under a slow-running stream of warm water. Avoid using forceful water pressure, which can drive contaminants deeper into the reel. Stubborn bits of dried mud and algae can be removed with a soft brush or rag.

Unless otherwise instructed by the manufacturer, never soak a reel for a prolonged period; many "sealed" drags and bearings are really water resistant rather than waterproof, and extended submersion can allow water to seep into these components, where it is slow to evaporate and increases the possibility of corrosion. Some drag materials—cork in particular—can absorb water and swell if they are immersed and left to sit. Rinse the spool thoroughly as well. You don't need to remove the line, though washing the reel is a convenient occasion to clean and dress the line.

Shake off the excess water, and use a soft cloth to wipe away any surface moisture. Then completely air-dry the reel and spool separately. You can speed up the drying time in a couple of ways, using a thin strip of lint-free cloth, for instance, to dry the spindle hole in the spool, since moisture there does not readily evaporate, and the cloth will pick up any dirt that hasn't rinsed away. Convenient as it might seem for the purpose, a cotton swab is not advisable for cleaning or drying the spindle hole. On some reels, this shaft sleeve contains clutch or needle bearings that can become contaminated with small fibers shed from the swab. And on many reels, the bottom end of this hole contains the spool-release mechanism, and cotton fibers left behind could affect its operation. When possible, and if the manufacturer does not recommend against it, you can also remove the screw that secures the handle to the spool and wipe it dry. Water trapped between the screw shaft and handle evaporates slowly.

Or you can take a different approach and simply use a hair dryer on a low-heat setting to speed things up, directing the air stream into the crannies and crevices that are difficult to wipe dry. Don't use a high heat, especially if the line is left on the spool; all you're aiming for is to expose the reel and spool to a stream of warm, dry air to evaporate any moisture in preparation for lubrication or storage.

Saltwater reels need more frequent and thorough cleaning; seawater can be murderously corrosive. And while most reels are manufactured from corrosion-resistant materials, it does not mean they are corrosion-proof. Aside from the oxidizing effects of the water, the dissolved minerals in salt water can produce an electrolytic reaction at the contact surfaces of components that are made of different types of metals, corroding the parts of the reel most directly involved in its mechanical operation.

The safest precaution is to wash a saltwater reel after each use. The procedure is similar to that for cleaning a freshwater reel—remove the spool, tighten or loosen the drag as recommended by the manufacturer, and rinse under slow-running warm water. Use a soft toothbrush to lightly scrub hard-to-reach areas—the joint between the reel foot and frame; ports in the spool and backplate; screw heads on the reel handle, reel foot, drag knob, spool hub, and line guard. Salt that is dried and trapped in cracks and crevices must be loosened and rinsed away. Again, it's not necessary to remove the line, but once you're standing at a sink with running water, you're halfway to washing the line anyway. Once you've rinsed the entire reel, shake off the excess moisture. Back off the pressure on the drag to its lightest setting, and carefully flush out the area beneath and around the drag knob on the reel exterior with running water. Then dry the reel as thoroughly as you can.

After a reel has been used regularly in salt water—say, after a week in the Florida Keys—or anytime the reel is to be stored for a while, it should be given a more thorough and scrupulous cleaning and then lubricated. The extent of this cleaning depends upon a couple of factors. First is the manufacturer's recommended procedure. Some reel makers, particularly those that use sealed drags or other sealed components, strongly discourage removing any internal parts of the reel for cleaning, in which case it's best to abide by the instructions. The second factor is how comfortable you feel in disassembling a reel. On reels with components that are easily removed, or designed to be removed by the owner, disassembly allows the most thorough cleaning. Most reels are relatively uncomplicated, and even partial disassembly allows access to components of the reel that may not be cleaned by simple rinsing. But if the idea of tearing down a reel seems a daunting one, a thorough washing with interior components in place will do.

Whether you disassemble it or not, a saltwater reel should be cleaned, as previously described, after extended use or prior to storage. Make liberal use of a soft brush on the frame, scrubbing the nooks and crannies that may still contain particles of salt even after daily rinsing. It's good practice, though few anglers undertake it, to strip the fly line and backing from the reel. Then scrub and rinse the spool, thoroughly cleaning the arbor, the ports or slots in the sides of the spool, and other areas that were covered up by the line and backing to make sure they are free of dried salts and minerals. (It's also good practice, and even less frequently done, to use this occasion to wash not only the fly line but the backing, as explained on page 96, to remove any contaminants that would be trapped against the spool surfaces for an extended period of time.) Finally, remove the screw holding the reel handle to the spool, and rinse both screw shaft and handle. Then dry everything thoroughly, and the reel is ready for any surface treatment, described below, and lubrication.

The most thorough cleaning of a reel—freshwater or salt—is obtained by stripping or partly stripping the interior of the reel, and washing the individual components and portions of the reel frame that are normally concealed. And indeed, some manufacturers recommend this approach. Unfortunately, the enormous variety of different reel designs makes specific, step-by-step instructions impossible. Nonetheless, there are some general guidelines and tips that are worth noting.

● Work on an uncluttered table or benchtop with plenty of light. Spread a terry-cloth towel over the work surface. If you drop any small parts—washers, screws, springs—the nap of the cloth will catch and hold them; on a hard surface, they tend to bounce into oblivion. Keep a paper and pencil handy; you may wish to jot down a few notes as an aid to reassembling the reel later.

● Use a multicompartment plastic box or an empty egg carton to hold the parts in sequence as you disassemble the reel.

- Reels that are designed to be dismantled for cleaning usually contain both disassembly instructions and a diagram of the interior components and their placement in the reel. Keep these instructions handy and visible. If you can't locate the instructions, some manufacturers post copies on their Web sites.

- Removing components on most reels requires only simple tools, and many require no tools at all for the recommended degree of disassembly. If tools are required, make sure they are properly sized for the task. An overly large or overly small screwdriver, for instance, can strip or damage a screw head and prevent retightening or future removal.

- Begin by removing the spool. Check the back face of the spool. Some designs may have a washer or even a gear that fits over the spindle, but it may be stuck to the back of the spool with grease or other lubricant. Remove any such parts, and beginning in the upper-left corner of the compartmented box, place each component in a separate compartment in the order in which it was removed.

- Continue disassembling the reel as indicated in the instructions, always watching for washers, bushing, or gaskets that may be sticking to other components with grease or oil. Be alert for components that have a "right-side up" and an "upside down." Some drag systems, for instance, employ gears or spring-type washers that must be replaced in the proper orientation for the reel to function. Jot down a note or sketch to indicate which side is which.

- In fact, I find it generally helpful to make notes or drawings as I go along as an aid to reassembling the reel. If you discover corroded parts that require attention, it may be a day or two before you put the reel back together, and the notes, along with any diagrams provided by the manufacturer, will help you reassemble everything properly.

- If any of the screws that secure removable components prove to be stubborn—the handle screw, for instance—from corrosion or some other cause, put a drop or two of penetrating oil or Liquid Wrench on the screw head, and give it time to bleed downward to the threads. If it still won't come free, leave it as it is.

- Take the reel down as far as you can, or as far as you care to go. Not all reels can be completely stripped of interior components—some may be riveted to the frame, or the manufacturer may discourage removing some parts. Or you may simply wish to leave some assemblies, such as pawl mechanisms, drag knobs, and so on, in place once the major drag components have been removed.

- Wash the components, one by one, replacing each in its proper compartment in the box or egg carton as you finish it. Remove dirt, grease, oil, and whatever gunk is clinging to them. While solvents won't harm metal parts, manufacturers tend to discourage them to prevent accidental contact with synthetic components. Some of these components, such as handles, drag knobs, and so on, are obvious, but some parts of the reel may contain synthetic washers, O-rings, and other components that are less conspicuous and potentially vulnerable to solvents. Solvents may also loosen the adhesive that holds a drag surface, such as cork, in place or damage matrix or impregnation compounds that are used in the drag material. Virtually all parts can be safely washed in warm, soapy water, scrubbed with a soft brush, and then rinsed. Dry them completely.

- Wash the frame completely, again using soapy water and a brush to get any saltwater residue that may be sticking to the reel frame or the parts remaining inside. Dry the frame thoroughly.

- Wash the spool. As indicated previously, the best method is to strip off the line and backing to get access to the whole spool. Unless the manufacturer advises against it, remove the screw securing the handle to the frame, and wash it. Dry all the components.

- At this point, you may wish to give the frame and spool a surface treatment for protection. Anglers I've known have used everything from a thin film of light oil, to Armor All, to automobile polish, all of which will provide some amount of surface protection. But a 15-year repair veteran I spoke with, who works on 3,000 reels a year, advocated a product—particularly for saltwater reels—called Boeshield T-9, an aerosol spray that contains corrosion protectants and waterproofing agents. It can be applied to the frame and spool inside and out, but avoid getting it on the fly line. Treatments like this can be sprayed directly on the reel or on a clean cloth for application to selected parts of the reel. If you choose any kind of surface treatment, avoid getting it on the reel handle or drag knob; these compounds can leave those surfaces extremely slippery.

- If you reassemble the reel at this point, take particular care in seating and tightening any screws that you've removed. Most screws secure into the reel frame or spool, which are typically made of aluminum. As metals go, aluminum is fairly soft. The screws are generally finely threaded, stainless machine screws that are quite hard. If the screw is initially misaligned and tightened with force, you could cross-thread the hole, which pretty much guarantees a trip back to the factory for repair. If the screw feels tight or resistant, back it out and try again. If everything is clean, it should go in easily.

Before reassembling the reel, however, you can take advantage of the fact that all the components are laid out and clean—a perfect time to perform an annual checkup and to lubricate the reel.

CHECKUP

Even if you faithfully perform routine maintenance, it's a good idea to check a reel over closely for any small problems that could cause bigger ones later. Of course there's little need to examine a reel closely for a bent frame or spool or other impact damage. Problems like these announce themselves all too clearly—a spool that won't rotate smoothly or sounds like a pepper mill when turned. But not all problems or potential problems are this obvious, and a close look at the reel is the only way to detect them.

It's best to check the reel after it's been thoroughly cleaned, just prior to lubrication; detecting damage or signs of corrosion is easiest on a clean surface. Inspect the exterior of the reel for any nicks or scratches that have penetrated the surface finish and show bright metal underneath. As explained below in the section "Repair," you may well choose to ignore surface damage that is essentially superficial, but deeper nicks, especially on saltwater reels, are worth attending to. Look closely at the palming rim on a spool with an exposed rim and the line guard, as these areas may require attention. A nick that has raised a burr on the edge of the spool can make palming the reel uncomfortable when you try to slow a hard-running fish. A burr or sharp-edged nick on the line guard is a high-priority repair, as it can abrade the fly line when you strip it from the reel. Note any such surface damage that requires attention.

As you inspect the frame and spool of a saltwater reel, be alert for any possible surface corrosion. Look closely at any "tight spaces"—the joint of the reel foot with the frame; the release mechanism on the spool hub; the ventilation ports in the spool and/or frame; screw or rivet heads.

If the reel is disassembled, inspect each part for rust, corrosion, pitting, or crystal-like buildups on the surface. If you haven't disassembled the reel, check the surfaces of the interior components as they are, in place, for rust or corrosion, paying particular attention to any screws, shafts, or other metal-to-metal contact points.

Inspect the spindle for any signs of rust or corrosion. These may appear as tiny pits or rough spots. Sometimes a light film of rust will form over the entire spindle, and it is so uniform in appearance that it may not be obvious that corrosion is setting in. A very faint brownish tint or a slightly powdery or grainy look to the surface of the metal may be your only clue. If you're in doubt, put a drop or two of oil on a clean rag; pinch it tightly around the spindle and rub fairly vigorously. If any rust-colored residue appears on the rag, the spindle will need attending to. Perform this same kind of check on the reel-handle screw.

Check to make sure all the screws on the exterior of the reel are tight—the screws that attach the reel foot to the frame, the handle to the spool, and the drag knob to the backplate. If your reel uses "pillar-and-frame" construction, where the backplate and front rim of the reel are joined by rod-type pillars with a screw at each end, check these as well. Screws used to assemble reels are not exactly the kind you find at a hardware store, and a lost screw virtually guarantees contacting the manufacturer for replacement. To check the screws, simply use a screwdriver to ensure that the screw is firmly seated. Don't screw it in tighter; just make sure it isn't loose. Again, make sure that the tool is properly sized to the screw head. If you've noticed screws that seem to loosen repeatedly, make a note of it along with any other problems or damage that needs attention, and see the "Repair" section below.

If the reel checks out okay, lubricate it.

LUBRICATION

One of the most important steps you can take to ensure long service and top performance of a reel is to lubricate it periodically. Lubricants decrease the wear on moving parts, promote smooth operation, and protect against corrosion. Conscientious lubrication is especially important on reels from which corrosion has been removed; previously corroded areas are particularly vulnerable to further attack. The frequency of lubrication depends on how regularly the reel is used, under what conditions, and how often it's washed, since repeatedly rinsing a reel even in plain water will remove some lubricant.

Freshwater reels need less meticulous attention in this respect; I clean and lube my own reels, for instance, at the end of each season to protect them during storage and ensure they will be in top operating condition for opening day. Lubricating a saltwater reel after each washing—which is to say, after each use—is probably overkill, but a quick lube after a week's worth or so of daily use is prudent. Anytime during the season the drag feels rough, stutters, or begins to squeak, it may need a touch-up. And again, it's certainly good practice to lubricate a saltwater reel at the end of the season when it will be stored for some time.

At this point, however, the matter gets a bit more complicated, since specific fly reels vary in design and materials, and reel makers differ in their recommendations about which parts of the reel should be lubricated and what lubricants should be used. Moreover, some reels are designed to be entirely self-lubricating and require only cleaning. The wisest course, as with cleaning a reel, is to consult and scrupulously observe the manufacturer's lubrication instructions, especially when it comes to drag mechanisms and friction surfaces, since certain types of lubricants are incompatible with certain drag materials. Still, there is enough common ground among reels to allow for some general guidelines and procedures.

SPINDLE. On a great many reels, the spindle—the shaft on which the spool turns—is simply a metal rod attached to the backplate, and lubricating it is an easy matter. Remove the spool and smear a light film of grease on the shaft. Don't apply it heavily; when the spool is replaced, you don't want excess grease squeezed into other parts of the reel. An all-purpose grease can be used, but many manufacturers recommend greases specifically formulated and sold for lubricating reels or products such as Super Lube, a Teflon-based grease. Replace the spool, and reel it forward a dozen times or so to distribute the lubricant over the spindle. Remove the spool again, and check to see if the grease has formed a film over the spindle right down to the base. If you've applied too much, wipe away the excess with a cotton swab.

SPOOL RELEASE. On many fly reels, especially freshwater types, the hub of the spool contains the spool-release mechanism, typically a spring-tension clip, operated with a small latch or button, that snaps into a groove on the spindle tip and holds the spool in place. The best way to lubricate this mechanism is to disassemble it. Most spool releases are concealed beneath a latch cover that is secured with small screws. If you wish to expose this mechanism, remove the screws, and lift the latch cover very slowly; some releases use tiny springs that can pop out if the cover is removed carelessly. If the release mechanism is dirty, clean it with water and a soft brush, and let it dry. Replace any components you've removed, apply a drop of oil such as Penn Lube, and screw the cover back on. Then operate the release a few times—by repeatedly flipping the lever or pushing the button—to spread the oil around.

If you don't wish to disassemble the latch, you may be able to use a fine-tipped dispenser to squirt a drop of oil into a space beside the latch lever or button that gives access to the interior of the release. Again, operate the release mechanism a few times to distribute the lubricant.

HANDLE. A bit of grease will keep the reel handle rotating freely on its shaft— usually a steel rod threaded on one end and screwed into the spool face. If possible or recommended (some manufacturers advise against it), unscrew this shaft and remove the handle; clean and dry it thoroughly if you haven't done so already. Smear a thin coat of grease over the shaft, and then reassemble the handle, seating the screw firmly, taking care as noted earlier not to cross-thread the screw.

If the handle on your reel is mounted in a way that prohibits disassembly, or you'd rather not remove it, you can oil it in place. Use a fine-tipped dispenser to place a small drop of oil on the screw-head end of the handle shaft. Spin the handle to work the oil inside the handle sleeve. Make sure to wipe away any excess to prevent the oil from making the reel handle slippery.

SPRING-AND-PAWL REELS. These mechanically simple reels employ a leaf or coil spring to apply pressure to the pawl (or on some reels, a pair of them), a metal or plastic tooth that engages a gear usually mounted on the inner spool face. This tooth-and-gear arrangement slows down the spool so that it doesn't overrun or backlash when line is stripped off; it also functions as the "clicker" on the reel. On some reels, the spring tension is adjusted with a knob on the backplate.

A few manufacturers recommend coating all the parts of this mechanism with grease, in which case those instructions should be followed. More typically, however, an oil such as Penn Lube is used.

Shown here is a typical spring-and-pawl system. Simply place a drop on all friction and contact surfaces—the shaft on which the pawl or pawls are mounted, the contact area between any adjustment knob and the reel frame, the point where the spring meets the pawl, and any pin or peg on which the spring is mounted.

DISC- OR ADJUSTABLE-DRAG REELS. Aside from lubricating the basic mechanical components—spindles, handles, and such—keeping the drag in smooth operating condition is the principal concern. But when it comes to adjustable-drag reels, there are so many different designs and materials that it is impossible to go much beyond a few generalizations. Some drags, most often those that incorporate friction surfaces made entirely of synthetic materials, are designed to be run "dry"—that is, without any lubrication at all. Lubricating them can cause the reel to misbehave severely. Other types of drags are sealed completely within a housing, and lubrication is not only unnecessary, but impossible. Again, at the risk of becoming tedious, I strongly advise consulting the manufacturer's specific instructions to determine if or how the drag should be maintained.

Some drags, though—typically those using cork as a friction surface—do require periodic lubrication, and the recommended lubricants vary. Some manufacturers advise using a light- or medium-weight oil, while others forcefully discourage (to the point of prohibiting) any petroleum-based lubricants for cork drags and recommend a Teflon-based grease such as Super Lube. If you are unsure, perhaps the safest course is to use neat's-foot oil, an animal-based product often used on leather and advocated by many reel makers. Neat's-foot oil does have lubricating properties, but it also works as a conditioner that keeps the cork elastic and water resistant and prevents it from drying out.

The cork drag surface is typically bonded to one face of the gear that fits over the spindle or attached to the interior of the reel frame itself. As a rule, the cork needs lubrication only if it sticks, chatters, squeaks, or feels very dry. To apply the oil, simply smear a thin film over the cork. Replace the spool, set the drag to a light tension, and strip off a few yards of line to distribute the lubricant and work it into the cork.

DRAG-ENGAGEMENT PIN. Some reels with an adjustable drag use a drag-engagement pin on the interior face of the spool. This spring-loaded plunger acts as a clutch, engaging the drag mechanism when the spool turns backward, but allowing the spool to rotate freely in the forward direction. Check the back side of the reel spool; if there's a small pin or peg near the center of the spool, press on it with your finger. If it springs in and out, the reel uses this drag-engagement design. Use a fine-tipped dispenser to place a small drop of oil on the pin. Then work the pin in and out to spread the oil, and wipe away any excess.

CLICKER. Some adjustable-drag reels have clickers mounted on the inside of the spool frame; others have it mounted on the inside face of the spool. Typically, these are very much like spring-and-pawl mechanisms, with a metal or plastic component held under spring tension against the teeth of a gear to produce the clicking noise. These are lubricated just as you would a spring-and-pawl mechanism.

REPAIR

NICKS, SCRATCHES, AND DINGS

Small nicks or light scratches that don't penetrate the surface coating of the frame or spool are essentially superficial and can be ignored. But if you wish to remove them for aesthetic purposes, you can try buffing them out with any of the commercial rubbing or buffing compounds used for automobile bodies. Frankly, this approach may or may not work, depending on the type of finish used on the reel and the depth of the scratch. But if cosmetics are important to you, it may be worth a try.

Surface damage that penetrates the exterior finish, especially on a saltwater reel, is worth attending to. Bare metal that is exposed to salt water can corrode. Fortunately, repairing this type of damage is fairly simple, and while the result may not win any trophies in the cosmetics category, it will protect the reel. The repair basically involves painting the exposed bare metal. I've tried various forms of "paint" with some success—enamel hobby paint, fingernail polish, and commercial metal paints—though with these, adhesion, chipping, and flaking can be a problem. What has worked the best by far is auto touch-up paint. It's widely available at automotive supply stores and service departments at car dealerships; it adheres extremely well and has surface toughness; and in addition to finding gloss black (which matches many fly reels), you may be able to locate it in other colors that are often used to finish reels such as gold, green, and gunmetal. And I have seen a clear version of this type of paint as well. Granted, you may not get a perfect match—touch-up paints dry glossy, while many reels are matte finished—but you can at least get close.

STEP 1: For this repair, determine whether the damaged area of the frame or spool has already corroded; if so, clean it up as explained below in "Rust and Corrosion." Otherwise, wash the bare metal and surrounding area with warm, soapy water and a soft-bristled brush, and rinse thoroughly. Then clean the nick or scratch with a rag dipped in a solvent such as acetone. The reel shown here hasn't been corroded, but it has a few chips, scratches, and spots of worn finish.

STEP 2: Apply a small amount of paint to the bare metal. To ensure complete coverage, the edge of the paint should extend onto the undamaged surface of the reel. For cosmetic purposes, you may want to keep the size of this paint patch to a minimum. For a thin scratch, try using a single, thick bristle from a 3- or 4-inch house-painting brush; a bristle like this has a nicely tapered end for precise application and is stiff enough to apply paint but still thin enough to remain largely within the confines of the scratch. If a nick or chip covers a larger area, use a small, soft brush to apply paint to the center of the damage and feather it a short distance onto the reel surface. Most touch-up paints have brush-top applicators that work well.

Here, the reel in the previous photo has had the exposed metal touched up with paint. (Incidentally, I used Toyota/Lexus "Phantom Gray" Touch-Up Paint #1E3 for this reel. It's a reasonably decent match for the gunmetal-gray Orvis Madison and Battenkill reels.)

Nicks or dings deep enough to reveal bare metal pose no real threat to most freshwater reels. The exposed aluminum (the material from which virtually all modern fly reels are made) will form a noncorrosive, oxidized coating, and the matter pretty much stops there. But as noted earlier, if an impact has raised a burr on the palming rim of the spool or a burr or sharp-edged nick on the line guard, you'll want to smooth it out.

STEP 1: To remove a burr or sharp-edged ding on the spool rim, as shown here, or on the line guard, it's best to strip off the fly line first. You can use a small, fine, round file to remove the raised metal. But make sure it's sharp; a dull tool is more apt to skate off a raised burr, increasing the risk of nicking an undamaged surface of the reel. Even so, you may want to mask off the spool with tape on either side of the damage to protect the surfaces.

An alternate approach is to use a round or conical medium-grit whetstone, dry or with a little honing oil smeared on it. The stone will cut more slowly, but gives better control, eliminating the stutter or chatter you can get with a file, particularly one that is too coarse.

STEP 2: File or stone the burr until it is nearly down to the level of the spool surface. Work slowly, with light strokes. Then file down the edges of the nick to feather the repair into the surrounding area. From the standpoint of function, all that's important is that the sharp edge be removed and the rim of the spool made smooth. If there's still a little roughness on the metal, use a hard

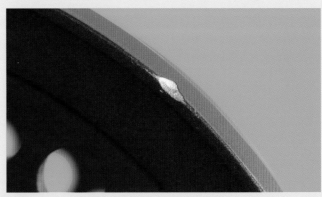

Arkansas stone to finish off the repair. On a saltwater reel, you should protect the bare metal, as explained above, with touch-up paint.

A nick in the line guard is repaired in exactly the same way, but it's best to paint the bare metal, even on a freshwater reel, to provide a smooth, nonabrasive contact surface with the line.

RUST AND CORROSION

If a reel has suffered from rust or corrosion, you may be able to clean it up and return it to operating condition depending upon the extent and location of the damage and—in the case of more extensive corrosion—your willingness to enter into a more involved process.

Corrosion or rust on the surface of a frame or spool is not terribly common on modern fly reels, though it certainly can occur on saltwater reels on which damage to the finish has exposed bare metal. To remove the corrosion, use a brush with stiff, synthetic bristles to scrub away any crystalline or grainy material. In more serious cases of corrosion, you may need to resort to a small wire brush or a Dremel-type tool fitted with a wire cup-brush or wire wheel to clean up the surface. Wire brushes should be used with care on the reel exterior to avoid scratching it, though such damage will probably just affect the appearance of the reel, and cleaning off the corrosion is the number one priority. When the area is free of residue, apply a protective coat of touch-up paint as explained previously.

The interior parts of a reel—freshwater or salt—are much more likely to have corrosion problems, and components made of steel are the most vulnerable. Steel is typically used for the spindle, drawbar components on reels that use this system, handle screws, and other small components such as springs, pawls, screws, and so on. There are two basic approaches to removing rust. The first is chemical treatment.

One of the simplest and most benign chemical removers is ordinary carbonated water. It won't affect synthetic materials, and you can safely soak the frame and components. You may, however, need to replace the soda water several times when it goes flat, and even then it tends to work best on very light rust.

There are a number of commercial chemical treatments designed to remove rust, and these are effective in eliminating heavier surface rust. CLR (calcium lime rust remover), often used in plumbing applications, is reasonably easy to find at plumbing supply houses and home improvement stores. Another product, Evapo-Rust, is nonirritating and biodegradable; it can be more difficult to find, though some auto parts shops stock it. And there are other liquid products on the market as well. As a rule, these rust removers call for immersing the affected surface for anywhere from 20 minutes to 24 hours, depending on the severity of the rust. Generally, these compounds won't damage plastics or other synthetic materials that may be used in reel construction (CLR, for instance, can be used to clean mineral deposits from coffeemakers). But I wouldn't soak a reel frame or any component that had a nonmetallic drag surface, especially cork, attached to it.

If, however, it is possible to dismantle the reel, chemical agents can be an effective way of removing rust, especially on components of the reel—screws, springs, and so on—that are small enough to make removing rust by hand difficult. Rather than using a compartmented plastic box to hold the disassembled components as you remove them, put them in a metal muffin tin instead. The chemical rust remover can then be poured selectively into the individual cups holding corroded components, allowing you to keep the parts in sequence for reassembly. If the frame has been stripped, it can be soaked as well to remove rust from the spindle or steel components permanently attached to the frame, always, of course, following the instructions provided with the specific chemical remover.

If the spindle is rusted, there may be a chance that there is corrosion as well in the spool hole where the spindle fits. On virtually all reels, this hole contains, at the very least, a bushing of a harder metal, such as bronze, since the aluminum itself is too soft for this high-wear surface. Bronze won't rust, though it can be subject to saltwater corrosion. On other reels, the spindle rides on ball or needle bearings inside the spool, and soaking a spool that houses bearings is a bit of a judgment call. But if there is visible rust on the bearings, or they are rusted to the point where they've frozen up, there seems little to lose in seeing if the corrosion can be chemically removed. The only other alternative is professional repair or replacing the spool.

After soaking the components, check to see that no rust remains. If the rust isn't completely gone, try soaking the components again. Once the components are clean, the reel can be reassembled. If the spindle was rusted and feels rough or grainy after the chemical treatment, you may wish to buff it with a polishing compound as explained below.

If you're hesitant about immersing a reel to clean rust from the spindle or interior components that can't be removed, you can try Naval Jelly. This compound is viscous, and, if applied to a surface, such as the spindle, it will adhere without dripping. Naval Jelly needs to be used very cautiously. It contains phosphoric acid, which can irritate skin and eyes; rubber gloves are recommended. And it can adversely affect some metals; it can, for instance, turn chrome-plated surfaces black, and it is not intended for use on aluminum. But it is an effective corrosion remover, and the gel-like consistency allows you to apply it precisely and locally on the interior of the reel.

If aluminum components—the reel foot or parts of the frame (or reel seats, for that matter)—are corroded, there is a similar product called Aluminum Jelly that is formulated to remove oxidation and the grainy "white rust" that sometimes forms on the metal. With both of these jelly compounds, it's better to use repeated, short applications of about five minutes, followed each time by rinsing in water, than one longer one.

If chemical treatments fail to do the job, or you'd prefer not to use them at all, you'll have to try the second approach, removing the rust by hand. This is, frankly, kind of an improvisational process; you use whatever works. Very fine sandpaper, steel wool, or emery cloth can be used to remove corrosion from the spindle or other surfaces. A wire brush is helpful in scraping corroded areas on irregularly shaped parts, such as gears.

One reel-repair expert told me that he finds a Dremel-type tool to be indispensable for this kind of work. He uses various attachments, small brush wheels and cylindrical cup-brushes, both synthetic and wire bristled, to remove corrosion from interior components, thoroughly cleaning off any loose or grainy material or deposits that are raised above the surrounding surface of the components.

The object is simple: get the part as clean as you can by scraping, brushing, and scrubbing. On spindles, which should be as smooth as possible, you can take one more step after the rust or corrosion has been removed. Using a Dremel-type tool, buff the spindle with a cloth wheel or drum and a polishing or rubbing compound or jeweler's rouge.

With persistence and a bit of resourcefulness, rust and corrosion can often be successfully removed.

The spring-and-pawl mechanism of the this freshwater reel was left wet for a prolonged period; you can see the accumulated rust on the springs, screws, and spindle.

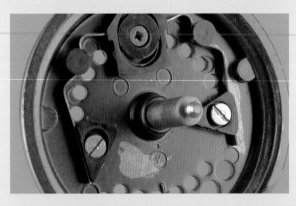

I cleaned the reel by first stripping it completely of interior parts and washing everything in warm, soapy water. All the parts (including plastic pawls and adjustment mechanism) and the frame were soaked in a solution of one part CLR to one part warm water for about six hours. Every hour or so, I used a stiff toothbrush to scrub the damaged areas to remove the surface rust and expose underlying corrosion to the CLR solution. After a thorough rinsing and drying, I used a Dremel tool with a wire wheel to remove the few remaining stubborn spots of corrosion. Touch-up paint was used to cover up a few nicks inside, and the reel was reassembled. A little lubrication and it will be ready to go.

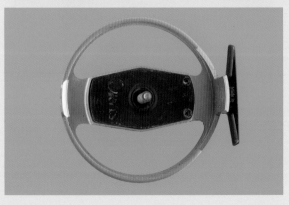

This saltwater reel was rinsed, with the spool removed, on a regular basis, and it looks to be in pretty good shape.

Unfortunately, the cover plate protecting the drag components wasn't removed when the reel was rinsed. Corrosion has set in and completely frozen the mechanism.

A combination of approaches was used to clean the reel. First, all the components were removed, except the plastic clicker arm. The shaft for the drag-adjustment knob (it's at the center of the hex nut) was frozen in place; a few treatments with Liquid Wrench eventually loosened it. Again, everything was washed in warm, soapy water.

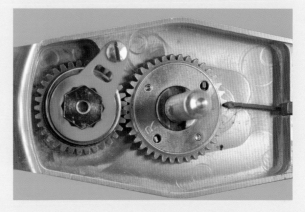

Since none of the removable components was aluminum, I used several applications of Naval Jelly to remove the corrosion. There were a few local areas of very heavy deposits, and while I'm certain that additional Naval Jelly would have removed them, when only small spots remained, I buffed them out with a Dremel tool and wire wheel or cup-brush.

There was an unidentified gummy substance on the interior of the frame—old grease, maybe. I removed it with lacquer thinner, then treated the frame interior with Aluminum Jelly, which took off most of the deposits. When it was clean, I could see that corrosion had pitted a few small areas on the frame; they appear here as dark spots near the edges of the gears. They shouldn't be a problem provided they are protected, and to finish this job, I'd use touch-up paint on the pitted areas, or at least keep them coated with a light film of oil or Boeshield.

As noted, there's not much you can do about surface pitting or etching on the reel frame or spool, and provided it's not too extensive, the reel should function fine. But if you discover that some interior components won't clean up or are corroded beyond recovery—especially small parts such as screws, washers, gears, or springs—your best course is probably to order replacement parts from the manufacturer.

Once you've repaired and reassembled a reel that has been subject to corrosion, it pays to be scrupulous about keeping it lubricated.

BENT FRAME OR SPOOL

Unfortunately, impact damage to the frame or spool that is severe enough to affect the operation of the reel can be difficult to repair, and though I've restored a handful of such reels to working condition, I've never been completely satisfied with the results. As a rule, a reel—particularly an expensive or valued one—with this kind of damage is best repaired by the manufacturer, who is more experienced and better equipped. Still, it can be done, and if the reel is of lesser value, or you damage a reel on a trip, you may wish to give it a try.

The first step is to isolate the specific area of damage. In some cases, it's obvious—you've dropped only the spool, or you can clearly see where the metal on the frame is deformed. Sometimes, though, it's less obvious whether it's the spool or the frame that has been damaged; all you can tell is that the reel scrapes or binds up when you try to use it. The quickest way to figure out where the damage lies, if you can, is to mount a spare spool on the frame. If the reel works properly, the original spool was damaged; if it continues to rub or scrape, the frame is the culprit.

If you don't have a spare spool, listen to the reel. If a reel with a single-sided frame makes a continuous scraping sound, it usually indicates damage to the frame; one of the frame members is bent and rubbing against the spool all the time. If the same reel only makes a noise at regular intervals as you turn the handle, it probably means a bent spot on the spool that is rubbing the frame members as it passes. On a reel with a full-cage frame, the noise it makes won't be a reliable guide, and you have to observe closely where the frame rim meets the spool to see if you can determine where the damage lies.

Fixing a bent frame or spool goes pretty much like you'd think; you try to bend it back into position with a pair of pliers.

One key is to figure out where the actual bend has occurred. On a spool, for instance, a bent edge may rub against the reel frame, but the location of the actual bend itself may be closer to the reel hub. Think of a flat lid removed from a coffee can. If you pinch one edge and pry it downward hard enough to bend it, you've obviously deformed the rim. But the bend itself is actually a straight crease across the lid, closer to the center. And this is the point on the spool you want to identify and bend back into position. Merely prying up the very lip of the spool will probably not fix the problem.

This same kind of thing occurs on frames; the bend that actually needs straightening may be located a short distance from the point where the frame rubs the spool.

A couple of points when using pliers: First, pad the jaws with a few layers of duct or electrician's tape to avoid marring the finish. Second, when working on spools, I've found slip-joint pliers to be the most useful. When closed, they have a hollow in the jaws, back from the tips, that allows you to reach and grab the face of the spool without pinching the spool rim itself, as shown here. You can thus position the jaws, and hence the leverage point of your efforts, at the site of the actual bend. Finally, work slowly and gently, frequently test-fitting the spool on the frame to see how you're progressing.

A different type of spool damage I've encountered more than once is a bit easier to repair. Many spools have a groove around the inside edge of the spool rim; the reel frame fits inside this groove. Dropping or hitting a spool on the edge can pinch this groove to the point where it rubs the frame. In this case, pad the blade of a flat screwdriver with tape. Insert it into the groove and work with a prying motion back and forth across the damaged area until the groove is opened wide enough to fit the frame.

LOOSE SCREWS

If you notice a screw on the reel that persistently comes loose during fishing, you can keep it secure and prevent its loss by using a thread-locking compound. There are two cautions here: First, use these compounds with an eye toward the future. A screw that should remain more or less permanently in place, such as the screws that attach the reel foot to the frame, require a more lasting treatment, such as Loctite 262 Permanent Threadlocker. On the other hand, screws that you may want to remove later on, such as the screw that secures the handle to the spool, should be dressed with a less permanent compound such as Loctite 242 Removable Threadlocker. In both cases, use threadlocker sparingly, and completely wipe off any excess that is forced out when you tighten the screw. And as noted earlier, use a screwdriver of the appropriate size to avoid damaging the screw head.

REPLACEMENT PARTS

Some types of damage cannot be repaired—a toe that breaks off the reel foot, a broken handle or pawl spring. Replacement parts are generally available from the manufacturer, sometimes for surprisingly old reels. An Orvis repair person, for example, told me that 99 percent of the time, he could furnish parts for reels manufactured as far back as 1970, and had at least some parts for reels even older. Other parts, such as worn drag surfaces or corroded components, can be also replaced and allow for refurbishing or even rebuilding a reel that you might otherwise consider a lost cause.

CHAPTER THREE

FLY LINES

O F ALL FLY-FISHING TACKLE, a fly line is the one most likely to meet a premature end. Though a line can certainly incur inadvertent damage that will render it useless on the spot, most lines don't suffer a sudden death. Rather, they die a little at a time. The casting, shooting, and handling properties gradually deteriorate. A floating line becomes more difficult to pick up cleanly off the water or to mend; it floats lower in the surface film or begins to sink, and nothing you do restores it to like-new performance. Finally, it all becomes annoying enough that you replace the line.

How long should a fly line last? It's impossible to attach precise numbers to the matter, but one thing is for sure—for many anglers, a fly line should last longer than it actually does. Though accidents may play a role, it is a small one. Far more often, carelessness and neglect hasten the demise of a line. I suspect that because the performance of an unmaintained line diminishes gradually, we grow accustomed to it as we fish and simply don't notice the decline in casting and handling characteristics, mistakenly thinking that the line is working just fine. But in fact a fly line requires more routine care than any other piece of equipment. Fortunately, it's also one of the easiest to maintain—and even simpler if you take a few basic precautions.

PREVENTION

- One of the single most common causes of serious physical damage to a fly line is stepping on it. Mud, grit, or sand ground against the surface of the line scores, or even cuts through, the exterior finish. Dirt becomes lodged in the small cracks, and larger ones admit water into the core of the line, both of which reduce buoyancy of a floating line. Stepping on the line can easily chew up the surface so that the line no longer slides smoothly through the guides, and casting distance is reduced. It can get even worse. From the back of a driftboat, I once watched the first 30 feet of a friend's fly line unroll, straighten out, and then fly off into the Madison River after he'd accidentally stepped on the line with a cleated wading boot and cut it in two.

When fishing from the bank, or in shallow wading, train yourself to carry loose line in coils in your hand, particularly when moving from spot to spot. When fishing from beaches or rock jetties, either hold excess line in coils or use a stripping basket to keep it from underfoot. If fishing from a driftboat or skiff, when line on the deck is almost inevitable, stand in a comfortable position to minimize shifting your feet, and get in the habit of looking down to check your slack line and make sure you're not standing on it. When casting from the deck of a flats boat, it's standard operating procedure, when possible, to fish barefoot (or wearing only socks, for sun protection) so you can feel if you step on the line.

Incidentally, one line expert told me that, contrary to popular opinion, casting a line on grass or even asphalt will not damage it (provided, of course, you don't step on it). It takes far more abrasive force to harm the coating, though a dry-cast line will become dirty.

- Don't leave a fly line in a closed vehicle or car trunk in warm weather or expose it unnecessarily to sunlight. Heat and ultraviolet rays accelerate the evaporation of plasticizers that keep the line supple and flexible, and the line will become stiff, brittle, and prone to cracking.

- Similarly, chemical agents can strip plasticizers from the line and, in extreme cases, even dissolve the coating itself. Keep lines away from contact with gasoline, petroleum-based compounds, sunscreen, and insect repellent (especially those containing DEET). If you apply sunscreen or bug dope, wash your hands before handling your line.

- When you're done fishing for the day, make one last, long cast. Then lightly pinch the line ahead of the reel in a handkerchief or even your shirttail, and reel it back on the spool. Algae and other surface contaminants are more easily wiped off when they haven't had a chance to dry, and cleaning the line later will be a simpler task.

- Under most circumstances, storing a line wet will not hurt it (though in humid tropical climates, it is possible for a line to mildew), but it's good practice to dry a line before spooling it (or in the case of a saltwater line, wash and dry it) to protect the reel from dampness that could corrode it.

- For long-term storage, lines (on or off the reel) should be kept in a cool, dark, dry place; in fact, a refrigerator or freezer is ideal.

CARE AND MAINTENANCE

Caring for a fly line both prolongs its life and maximizes its performance, and in maintaining a line, the unequivocal, hands-down, top priority is keeping it clean. Most floating lines float because the coating surrounding the core contains hollow microbubbles that make the line lighter than water. Moreover, line coatings usually contain a hydrophobic agent that repels water so that the line rides high in the water rather than becoming swamped in the surface film. A high-floating line is easier to pick up off the water and to mend.

Contaminants on the surface of the line have various consequences, all of them bad. Algae or other material suspended in the water and transferred to a floating fly line forms a barrier between the water and the hydrophobic finish on the line; the line won't repel water as well and won't float as high. Surface contaminants also increase friction between the line and guides, and a dirty line—floating or sinking—will not cast as smoothly, as easily, or as far as a clean one. More importantly, when the line drags against the guides, the surface coating is stretched slightly, and repeated stretching of this type can cause cracks to develop. Third, dirt, salt, silt, or tiny of particles of sand adhering to the line essentially form a film of gritty, abrasive material on its surface. The constant rubbing of the line against the guides when casting or fighting fish will cause wear on the fly-line coating and even on the rod guides.

This kind of friction from a dirty line also explains a very common experience among freshwater anglers, who tend to make many more casts in a day than saltwater fly fishers—lines that wear out in one spot. Most of us have a preferred, comfortable casting distance—say, 35 feet. We make a cast, and strip in slack as it develops. When we pick up to make another presentation, we work out the slack during false-casting, and then make another cast of approximately the same distance as the first. The result is that the same section of the line is worked back and forth repeatedly through the guides, over and over, and on a poorly maintained line, this section will become slightly rough or tend to sink or wear out, even though the rest of the line is in good condition.

It's worth pointing out that "cleaning" a line and "dressing" it are two different procedures, though informally we often interchange the terms. That's not a problem provided we understand the difference, particularly that the latter is not a substitute for the former. Cleaning, as explained below, is a matter of removing surface dirt. Dressing, as explained later, involves treating the surface of the line. When dressing is applied to a dirty line, some dirt may appear on the cloth or applicator, but this is only an incidental side effect of dressing. As a way of cleaning a line, it is neither very complete nor very effective.

CLEANING

How often a fly line needs cleaning depends a great deal on the water you fish. In relatively clean water, a line doesn't pick up a great deal of surface contamination, and you may fish it over the course of several trips before it needs washing. A line fished in muddy, turbid, or heavily alga-laden water may need cleaning every day. According to one industry expert, there's very little risk in overwashing a line. Mild soaps remove little of the line plasticizer, and the potential damage or premature wear that you risk by fishing a dirty line is by far the greater concern. The fact is, most anglers do not wash their lines frequently enough and often don't even think about it at all until line performance has noticeably deteriorated or the line is visibly dirty. At that point, damage may already be done. The tendency to overlook or postpone cleaning a line is most apt to happen when it's new. The performance of the fresh line is so superior to that of the old one that cleaning it never occurs to the angler until the line becomes so dirty that performance starts to suffer.

Moreover, a dirty line attracts even more dirt; material adhering to the line provides a rough surface that traps and holds additional contaminants. And the dirtier a line gets, the more trouble it is to clean.

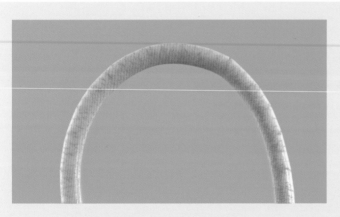

A badly neglected line often develops tiny, dark, hairlike lines on the coating; these are actually tiny cracks that have become filled with dirt. It is impossible to get them clean. The tension put on the line during normal casting and fishing tend to stretch the coating, and these cracks only get bigger with use, compromising line performance and shortening its life.

As noted earlier, a line that is repeatedly fished when it is dirty can suffer surface abrasion. It may be so finely abraded that you can't actually feel it with your fingers, but even if you wash the line, the rough surface provides a foothold for new dirt, and keeping it clean is tedious.

When most anglers think about cleaning a line, they tend to think of the floating type. But don't overlook your sinking and sink-tip lines; they will profit from washing as well. A clean line simply casts better than a dirty one, and on intermediate and slow-sinking lines, a clean surface penetrates the surface film more rapidly and uniformly.

Perhaps the best advice is to clean your lines more often rather than less, even if the line is new, and avoid letting it become so dirty that its casting and handling characteristics are irrevocably diminished and its usable life shortened. All synthetic lines can be cleaned with warm, soapy water. Avoid detergent products, though, since they can be very aggressive in stripping plasticizer from the line. Use a mild hand soap. It isn't necessary to wash the entire line, only that portion that regularly comes into contact with the water. For a trout fisherman, it may only be the first 35 or 40 feet of the line; for a saltwater angler, it may be twice that. Different anglers have different methods for washing a line, but in the end, it comes down to the same thing—wiping down the surface of the line.

The easiest way I have found is to wash lines at a double sink, since the two basins provide convenient containers for holding the line and preventing tangling, and rinse water is right at hand. Strip off the amount of line you want to wash, and place it carefully in one of the sink basins. Laying the line down in an orderly fashion in the sink will help prevent tangling. Then strip off an extra 6 feet or so, and place the reel well out of harm's way. Leaving this extra slack helps prevent you from accidentally jerking the reel with a taut line and knocking it to the floor during washing. Since the end of the line nearest the reel is at the top of the pile of the line in the basin, begin washing at that end. Pinch the line lightly in a soapy cloth, and simply draw an arm's length of line through the cloth. Then place that section of the line in the second, empty sink basin. Continue drawing lengths of line through the cloth, laying them carefully in the other sink until you reach the tip of the line where the leader is attached. Then repeat the process, beginning with the tip of the line this time, drawing sections of the line through soapy cloth and laying them in the first sink basin. Continue repeating until no more dirt appears on the cleaning cloth.

Don't scrub the line vigorously or pinch it very tightly in the rag. Think of cleaning the line as you would washing a dirty car; overly aggressive rubbing of surface dirt turns a cleaning rag into a piece of sandpaper that will scratch the finish.

I do, however, like to give extra attention to the first 2 or 3 feet at the tip of a floating fly line. Since the line tapers toward the tip, the coating that provides buoyancy is thinnest in this section. There's less flotation in this part of the line, and dirt has a corresponding greater effect, causing the tip to sit awash in the surface film or to sink.

After the line is clean, rinse it thoroughly, drawing lengths of the line through a stream of warm water running from the faucet and placing them in the empty side of the sink. I usually repeat the process another time or two to make sure that all the soap has been removed. Once the line is rinsed, draw it through a dry cloth as you spool it back on the reel.

Some lines are designed be to cleaned with a special cleaning pad containing a micro-abrasive that will remove surface dirt without harming the line itself. Such pads can be used wet or dry, but it's important to determine if this method is recommended by the manufacturer. Most lines, including Orvis Wonderlines, will be damaged by using this kind of pad or any abrasive cleaner. The cleaning process is the same as described above, drawing lengths of line through the pad until no more residue appears. Rinsing is not necessary.

You may find it necessary to clean your line at some point during a day's fishing if a floating line is riding too low in the water or beginning to sink. You can put a cloth damp with soapy water in a zip-closing bag, and tuck it in your vest. Then cast the line out and strip it back through the cloth two or three times. You can even do a passable job washing the line with drinking water and a clean rag, though a more thorough cleaning is probably in order afterward. There are also some combination "cleaner/conditioner" or "cleaner/dressing" compounds available that can be used onstream to clean lines even if they are wet. In my experience, these compounds do a better job dressing than they do cleaning, but you will quite probably notice some temporary improvement in the line performance from the dressing alone. Again, though, a thorough cleaning at the end of the day is a good idea.

Once the line is clean, you may wish to dress it.

DRESSING

The truth of the matter is that many modern fly lines, particularly those formulated with extremely slick, smooth surface finishes, rarely need dressing or don't need it at all. Other lines, however, profit from periodic dressing, and as always it's best to consult the manufacturer's specific recommendations. Applying a dressing compound lays a thin film on the exterior of the line that makes the surface slicker and smoother, and helps restore its hydrophobic properties. A dressed line also tends to tangle less, a particular concern in saltwater angling when a significant quantity of line may lie on a boat deck or in a stripping basket, in readiness for a long cast or as slack from retrieving a fly. When piled-up coils of fly line run out, from shooting line on a double haul or from a running fish, they are prone to tangle when one coil rubs another and "grabs" it—which happens more often with a soft, sticky, dirty line. A dressed line is smooth and slippery, reducing the possibility of a tangle and decreasing the risk of a blown cast or a lost fish.

Virtually all line manufacturers sell or recommend a specific type of line dressing. Orvis, for instance, advises using Zip Juice, which is designed for its Wonderlines but works very well on most lines. A great many of these products are silicone based and provide a slick, reasonably long-lasting treatment. Some anglers advocate the use of conditioner/protectant products such as Armor All, and provided these products contain no solvents, there's little chance that they will harm a fly line. The problem is that they are often water based and tend to wash off lines fairly quickly, making more frequent applications necessary. Using a longer-lasting dressing specifically formulated for fly lines just makes more sense. Compounds containing solvents should never be used. Dressings of this type, such as the old-fashioned Mucilin paste, will cause a line to become stiff and brittle. Be aware that some line dressings are most effective if they are allowed to dry—sometimes as long as 24 hours—before fishing; such information can be found on the label. It is worth heeding and planning for your line dressing accordingly.

Since a line is dressed to improve its slickness, shooting and handling, and water-repelling properties, the frequency of dressing depends on how well those characteristics of the line are maintained. Even silicone-based dressings eventually wash or wear off, and when you notice a decline in the performance of the line, it may be time to treat the surface again. Climate and fishing application also have their effects. A line that is cast and fished continuously in warm weather will need more frequent dressing than one used in colder temperatures or one that lies idle on the deck most of the day, waiting for a shot at a permit or bonefish.

To dress a line, follow the specific product instructions. Typically, dressing involves applying a small amount of the compound to a clean cloth and drawing the line through it. When possible, I prefer to dress a line in much the same way I wash it—in a clean, dry double sink. This prevents piling loose line on the floor, where the wet dressing can pick up dirt or debris. Many manufacturers recommend that the line be buffed with a dry cloth after the dressing is applied to distribute the compound evenly, remove any excess, and polish the surface of the line. But whether buffing is recommended or not, it is best to use line dressing sparingly. Excess dressing on the line can actually pick up contaminants from the water and diminish, rather than improve, performance in exactly the same way that overdressing a dry fly with paste floatant can cause it to sink.

If you need to dress a line onstream, choose a dressing that can be used on wet lines and doesn't require drying time. Try to pick a grassy area on which to lay down the loose line to avoid getting it dirty, and strip off the amount of line you wish to dress. Hold the line, just ahead of the rod grip, in a cloth treated with floatant, and reel the line back onto the spool. In a pinch, you can simply make a cast on the water and retrieve the line through a cloth treated with dressing.

Though the practice does vary among anglers, I like to dress full-sinking lines to improve their casting and shooting performance. The exception here is intermediate lines and other low-density, slow-sinking types. The hydrophobic properties of the dressing can cause such lines to hang up in the surface film or sink erratically; they should, however, still be washed. The sinking portion of a sink-tip line is generally short enough so that it is already beyond the rod tip when the angler false-casts or casts, and dressing it serves no real purpose, though dressing the floating portion of the line is advisable. Floating running lines that are used with shooting heads can be cleaned and dressed as well, though take care to wipe off any excess dressing and, if possible, let the running dry. You don't want dressing migrating to a sinking shooting head when the running line and head are packed together on the reel spool.

BACKING

Most anglers, particularly those who pursue trout and warmwater species, pay little attention to their backing. They tend to see it once, when they spool it up, and maybe once again, perhaps years later, when they remove or replace it. In most circumstances, this is a matter of little consequence. Modern backings—usually Dacron or gel-spun poly—are remarkably resistant to rot, mildew, and deterioration, and they retain their strength for quite some time.

Backing used for saltwater fishing, however, is a different story. Though it is not subject to greater deterioration, it does tend to see a good deal more use; big, hard-running fish can expose much of the backing to salt water. Unlike the smooth coating of a fly line, the surface of the backing is textured and can readily accumulate tiny particles or sand, grit, and dried salt. But even backing that spends most of its time on the spool still gets wet from spray and from water transferred from the fly line, and when the backing dries, tiny salt crystals are left behind. Backing that is wet with salt water can promote corrosion on the reel spool. An undamaged spool, with the surface finish intact, is relatively safe, but a nick or scratch that has penetrated to bare metal on the arbor or the interior of the spool or anyplace that contacts the backing offers an entry point for corrosion.

A more common problem occurs when dirty backing slides against the guides, particularly under pressure from a running fish. The contaminants essentially turn the backing into a thin, flexible, abrasive string that can produce wear, or even grooving, on the guides of a heavily used rod.

The best solution is to wash the backing periodically. Few anglers seem to actually bother with this, though according to a rod-repair person I spoke with, more of them should. There's no really convenient way to wash backing because there is so much of it. And unlike the comparatively stiff fly line, the backing is limp, and merely piling it in a heap can produce nightmarish tangles. Even so, washing fly-line backing that sees regular use in salt water is a good idea.

I have never found a really good way to wash backing, though I have found a few bad ones. The double-sink method used for washing lines puts too much backing into too small a space for tangle-free handling. I've tried stripping backing into a bathtub of water, but any disturbance of the water—an accidental swishing or turning on the tap—tends to wash the coils together into a mess.

These days, I use the backyard. Beginning in one corner, I strip off fly line as I walk along, laying it down in a straight line. When I reach the limits of the lawn, I reverse directions, continuing to strip line and then backing, laying it down parallel to, and about a foot away from, the line already on the ground. I continue walking back and forth, laying the backing down in parallel lines, making sure that it never crosses itself. I try to plan this little stroll so that I end up at the hose bib with an empty reel. Then I turn on the faucet and retrieve the backing onto the reel through a slow stream of water, pinching it to squeegee off any dirt and excess moisture. It's a bit involved, but it works, and fortunately it does not need to be done often.

LINE TWIST

A fly line that has become twisted isn't a maintenance problem in the sense of causing damage, but it's certainly a performance-related issue. It's easy to tell when a line is twisted; slack line between the stripping guide and the reel that would normally hang downward in a simple U shape instead wants to twist around itself, or "furl." You must pull out this twist before you can work out slack line during false-casting, which is a nuisance. And if you try to shoot slack that tends to furl, it will rob distance from your cast or even jam in the stripping guide.

Line twist has a couple of causes, and the first is improperly mounting the line on the reel. After the line has been attached to the arbor of the reel or to the end of the backing, don't lay the line spool flat on a table or on the floor and simply wind line onto the reel. Pulling line off the face of the spool automatically introduces twist.

Instead, run a pencil through the center of the line spool; have someone hold the ends of the pencil horizontally, so that the line spool is vertical, as shown here. Notice orientation of the spool and reel: the line comes off the bottom of the line spool to the bottom of the reel. You can lightly pinch the line as you reel it up to provide a little tension.

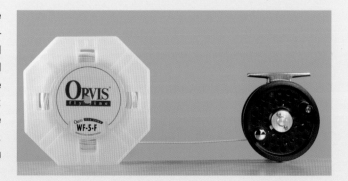

Line twist can also accrue as a result of some casting motions. When many anglers cast, the tip of the rod does not travel in a straight line. Rather, it takes a slightly elliptical path; if a right-handed caster looked up at the rod tip, it would be traveling counterclockwise through a narrow oval. (For a left-handed caster, it would be clockwise.) Over time, twist will develop as a result.

The simplest way to remove twist is to strip off 20 or 30 feet of line (a leader attached is fine, but no fly), and let it trail downstream in an evenly paced current of moderate speed or troll it slowly behind a boat or float tube. Reel it in, and the twist will be gone. Or you can strip out 15 or 20 feet of line and keep it aerialized, if you are right-handed, by moving the rod tip through a clockwise oval (as viewed when looking up at the tip) for 15 or 10 revolutions. (Lefties should go counterclockwise.)

CHECKUP

From time to time, you should inspect your line—that is, the forward part of the line that gets regular use—to make sure it's in good condition. And as with all tackle, detecting problems is easiest when the line is clean.

Strip the desired amount of line off the reel, laying it down neatly. With your left hand, draw the line slowly through your right thumb and forefinger, perhaps 6 or 8 inches at a time, looking and feeling for any rough spots, abrasion, cracks, or other exterior damage. I usually use my left fingers to roll the line back and forth as I pull in order to see all around the perimeter of the line. (Don't continually roll it in one direction or you will introduce twist into the line.) If I find any surface damage, I flag it with a piece of masking tape, and continue on.

Pay particular attention to the last few inches at the tip of the fly line. If you attach your leader with nail knot, inspect the line immediately adjacent to the knot. Over time the knot can bite into the coating of the line, and the repeated hinging of the flexible fly line against the hard knot can cause a crack to develop in the line coating. A crack can expose the core of the line, which will absorb water and reduce the buoyancy of the line tip. On a saltwater reel, you may want to strip all the line off and inspect the backing knot as well. Fly lines that have a braided loop mounted on the end for attaching the leader are less prone to this hinging and cracking, but they are still worth looking at closely.

If, after inspecting the line, you've detected any surface damage, you may want to consider whether it's worth attending to, as explained in the next section. But finally fly lines do have a finite life span, and even with scrupulous care, they will wear out. A line that has developed large areas of surface roughness, or is riddled with dark microcracks, or has lost its flexibility and feels stiff and brittle, or simply casts poorly no matter what you do is probably nearing the end of its days.

REPAIR

Though there is no real way to restore a line that has been badly neglected or is worn out, smaller local repairs can extend the life of the line, improve its performance, or return it to fishable condition.

TIP DAMAGE

If the line is cracked or abraded adjacent to a nail knot or other line/leader connection, simply trim away the damaged portion and reattach the leader. Losing a few inches of the fly-line tip will not noticeably affect its casting behavior. Repeatedly trimming back the tip or cutting away a damaged section farther back from the tip, however, can alter the casting properties of the line, depending on the specific taper. How much of the tip can be removed and still give a line that performs satisfactorily depends on how much change in the casting characteristics an angler is willing to tolerate. Many modern lines have level tips about 6 to 12 inches long. Once this level section is removed, the taper is shortened and the tip of the line is thicker. Generally, the line will have a more powerful delivery but reduced delicacy when it lands on the water.

SUPERFICIAL CRACKS AND ABRASIONS

Some types of surface damage to the line, small cracks or localized abrasions, are essentially superficial, which is to say that they are shallow enough that the core of the fly line is not exposed. If that's the case, there is no real functional purpose in repairing the damage since the core is still protected and cannot absorb water.

If, however, you wish to repair the area—for cosmetic reasons or, in the case of a small crack, to prevent it from widening and exposing the core—you can patch the area with a flexible adhesive, such as Aquaseal. It produces a fairly durable repair, though ultimately a temporary one. Eventually, with continued flex and stretch of the line, the bond between the adhesive and the line will weaken; the patch will peel off and require replacement. But the basic repair is not difficult.

As noted in Chapter 4, where Aquaseal is used extensively in patching waders, I recommend the use of Cotol-240 Cure Accelerator whenever this adhesive is used. The accelerator shortens the drying time significantly, and in the following repair, it minimizes the time spent tending the line to eliminate dripping and sagging of the adhesive patch.

To mend an abrasion in the fly line, shown at the top, first thoroughly clean the damaged area and a short section of intact line on either side of it. You want to remove any surface contamination and old line dressing. Let the line dry completely. In this type of repair, it helps to have the line elevated above the work surface and drawn taut. An easy way to accomplish this is to sandwich the line between two stacks of heavy books and then pull the line taut. It doesn't need to be bowstring tight, but you do want a reasonably immobile surface on which to apply the adhesive. The damaged area of the line should be centered and facing upward, as shown at the top.

The damage should be patched with a flexible adhesive. A rigid glue will produce a "hard" spot in the line, and repeated flexing and stretching of the line during fishing will cause it to flake off fairly quickly. Aquaseal works well for this repair. To apply the adhesive, shave the end of a wooden toothpick at an angle to produce a flat surface that you can use as a tiny spatula.

Put a very small amount of Aquaseal on the end of the toothpick and spread it into or over the damaged area, extending the patch a short distance outward to the intact line on either side. The goal here is to fill in a nick, seal a crack, or smooth out a rough spot without leaving a bulky layer of adhesive on the line. Once the adhesive is applied, moisten your fingertip and run it lightly back and forth across the patch; the water will prevent the glue from sticking to your finger as you smooth out the surface of the Aquaseal, as shown at the bottom.

As the patch is drying, check it periodically for the first hour or so to see if the Aquaseal is sagging to the underside of the line, producing a drip. If so, rotate the line so that the drip is facing upward; gravity will cause the adhesive to level out. Let the patch dry thoroughly.

DEEP NICKS AND ABRASIONS

Localized surface damage that is deep enough to expose the core of the fly line should be repaired, particularly on a floating line. The line core will absorb water, and the damaged portion of the line may begin to sink. Moreover, when water enters the line, it weakens the adhesion of the coating to the core, and the coating adjacent to the damaged area may itself fail and separate from the core. The damaged area becomes larger, leading to further coating loss, and so on. So timely attention is wise.

Deep nicks or abrasions can be repaired in exactly the same way as you'd repair superficial damage, by applying Aquaseal, though in this case, after washing the damaged area, give the line core ample time to dry completely. You don't want to seal any water inside the line, and if the exposed portion of the core is damp, the Aquaseal won't adhere well.

SEVERED COATING

Sometimes a deep cut or slice severs the fly-line coating all the way around the line right down to the core. This type of damage typically occurs when the tippet gets tightly snared or knotted around the fly line and bites through the coating.

A cut like this can be repaired with an Aquaseal patch, as explained above. But under tension, the cut ends of the core will tend to separate, and a surface patch is more likely to lose its grip. Provided the core is undamaged, there's no real risk of the fly line actually breaking should the ends of the coating separate; the strength of the line is in the core. But a better repair can be effected by getting some adhesive on the exposed ends of the coating, bonding them to one another and to the core as well to prevent water from entering and to prevent the gap between the ends of the coating from getting wider.

I've used Aquaseal, gel-type super-glue, and flexible CA glues such as Loctite 414 and Flex-Zap for this repair with good results.

Wash and dry the damaged area thoroughly. Gently fold the fly line, as shown, to widen the cut and expose the core. Take a small bit of adhesive on the tip of a toothpick, and apply it to the gap between the coating ends. Get some 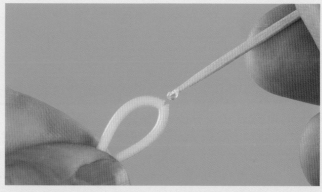 adhesive on the cut ends of the coating and on the core.

Straighten the line out, rotate it 90 degrees, and gently fold it again to expose another section of the cut. Apply more adhesive. Continue rotating, folding, and gluing until you've applied adhesive to the entire cut surfaces of the coating and core between them. Then straighten out the line; if any adhesive is squeezed out on the surface of the line, remove as much as you can with a toothpick, and use a moistened finger to spread the remainder over the surface of the line as smoothly as you can. Then push the cut ends together, and hold for a few minutes until the glue begins to set. Let the patch dry completely.

SPLICING

Sometimes a longer length of fly line becomes abraded; it gets wrapped around a rock or coral head or hung up in an oyster bed and seesaws over a sharp surface under the exertions of a fish or an angler. A length of the line becomes surface damaged to the point where casting is impeded or the core is exposed in several places. How you repair such damage is something of a judgment call. It is certainly possible to repair it with a coating of Aquaseal, as described above, though over longer lengths of line the coating must be applied in stages, and you will end up with a length of fly line that, while not rough in texture, has an uneven surface and may be stiffer than the rest of the line. Under these circumstances, some anglers choose to cut away the damaged section entirely and splice the line back together.

There are downsides to this approach. It's a more involved type of repair, though it is not especially difficult. And depending on the specific area and extent of the damage, it can also change the casting behavior of the line. If the damage spans a tapered portion of the line, and that section must be removed, you can alter the taper in a variety of ways—shortening the front or back end of the head on a weight-forward line, or introducing an abrupt step in taper on a double-taper line. And again, whether the repaired line will cast satisfactorily depends on how much change in casting performance an individual angler is willing to accept. Splicing a level section of the taper or a running line will affect the casting performance far less, or not at all.

Splicing, however, has some advantages over a surface repair. It eliminates the potentially long, uneven surface of an adhesive repair, and replaces it with a more localized and unobtrusive patch that many anglers feel handles better. A splice is more permanent; correctly done, it should not need replacing. And of course, a splice is the only repair possible in some circumstances—if the line is cut completely in two, or abrasion has been so extensive that the core of the line itself is damaged or frayed and actual breakage is a possibility.

Two approaches to line splicing are demonstrated below, and a third one is simple enough to perform on the water that it is explained in the section "Field Fixes."

NEEDLE SPLICE. The needle splice involves threading the core of one piece of fly line into the core of the other and securing it with glue. It forms a neat joint, but it can only be used to splice fly lines that have braided, not mono, cores. I've seen various types of adhesives recommended, but I think the best is a flexible glue such as Loctite 414, a cyanoacrylate adhesive designed for use on plastic and vinyl, or Flex-Zap. Both have good bonding strength and remain somewhat flexible when they dry, minimizing the "hard spot" at the splice that can cause the line to hinge and eventually fracture the coating.

For the needle splice, you'll need:
- A sewing needle at least 1½ inch long
- A razor blade
- A pin vise (sold at hobby shops) or needle-nose pliers
- A foot-long piece of Kevlar tying thread or dental floss
- Flexible CA glue

STEP 1: Cut away any damaged section of the line. With the razor blade, trim the sections of the line so that the butt ends are square.

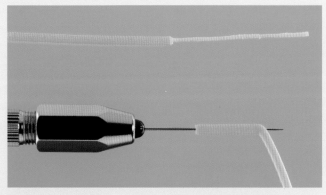

Strip about 1½ inches of the coating from the end of one of the line sections to expose the core, as shown at the top. You can remove the coating by using the razor blade to make a shallow cut into the coating all the way around the line; don't go so deep, however, that you nick or damage the core. Then pull the coating at the tip of the line; with enough force, the coating will break at the cut and peel off the end, leaving the core intact, as shown at the top. If you have difficulty stripping the coating, try working at it in increments of ½ inch or so rather than trying to remove the whole section at once.

As an alternative, you can tie a piece of tippet material with an overhand knot around the line at the strip-off point. Seat the knot tightly, then pull the tag ends of the tippet firmly toward the tip of the fly line and strip away the coating.

Mount the needle in the pin vise (or grip it in the pliers), and insert the point into the core of the unstripped section of line. The idea here is to work the needle through the center of the fly-line core for a distance of about an inch. You may find it helpful to dull the needle point to prevent it from catching on the weave of the core material, which can force the needle off center inside the line.

When an inch or so of the needle is inserted into the fly-line core, bend the line around the tip of the needle, and push the needle so that it pierces through and exits the fly-line coating, as shown at the bottom.

Since you'll be pulling the exposed core of the other section of line through the passageway you've made with the needle, you want this passage to be as wide as possible. Here are a couple of tips: Choose a needle that is about the same diameter as the exposed fly-line core. Bigger is in fact better, but the larger the diameter, the more difficult it is to work the needle through the middle of the fly line. Once the needle has been fed through the line and pierced through the coating, work it back and forth, twist it, slide the "sleeve" of fly line up and down the needle. Or you can remove the needle, and temporarily insert one of an even larger diameter to help enlarge and hollow out the center of the fly line. The bigger the passageway, the easier it will be to pull the core material through.

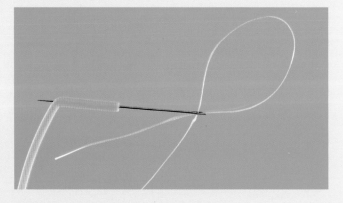

STEP 2: Remove the pin vise. Fold the Kevlar thread or dental floss in half, and thread both tag ends a short distance through the needle eye.

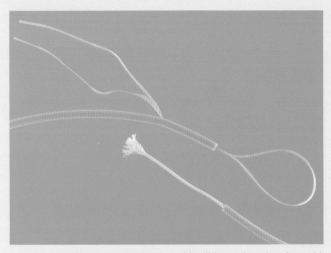

STEP 3: Mount the tip of the needle in the pin vise (or grasp it with the pliers), and pull the eye of the needle through the core of the fly line and out the exit hole, drawing with it the two tag ends of the thread. Remove the needle and pull the thread ends so that the loop of thread at the tip of the fly line is about 1 inch long, as shown here at the top.

Now use the needle to fray the first ¼ inch or so of the exposed core on the second section of line, as shown at the bottom. You'll be using the thread loop to draw the exposed core through the center of the fly line; the frayed end gives some bulk and grip inside the loop so that the core material doesn't slip out when you're pulling.

STEP 4: Slip the frayed end of the core into the thread loop. Pull on the thread tags to snug the loop against the end of the fly line, as shown.

Coat the exposed core with adhesive, and put some glue on the cut faces of the fly-line sections.

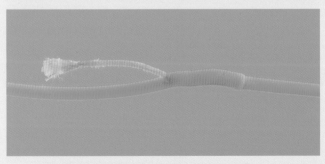

STEP 5: Working quickly, pull the thread tags, drawing the exposed core material inside the intact fly line until the core material comes out the exit hole in the line coating and the two ends of the fly-line sections abut one another firmly. You may need to use a pair of hemostats or pliers to grasp and pull the thread tags. This process can go easily or not, depending primarily on how large you've made the passageway through the fly line. Put a drop of adhesive right at the point where the core material exits the coating.

STEP 6: When this drop of glue is dry, use the razor blade to trim the tag end of the core material flush with the surface of the fly line. Test the splice by pulling on it—quite hard—to make certain the glue bond is secure. Here is the finished splice.

Some anglers prefer to coat the joint with a thin film of Aquaseal as explained on page 99. If the two spliced sections were of different diameters, there will be a "ledge" at the joint. A tapered coating of Aquaseal over the joint will make a smooth transition from one section of the line to the other.

GLUE SPLICE. The second approach to joining two sections of fly line, the glue splice, was shown to me by Al Buhr, an expert fly caster from Oregon who devised the technique for constructing custom spey lines, and I'm indebted to him for sharing it. The method results in a short, fairly flexible splice that is quite durable; works on fly lines with both braided and mono cores; and, provided you have the right adhesive, can even be performed streamside. Buhr prefers Loctite 414 for the purpose.

For a glue splice, you'll need:
- A sharp knife (an X-Acto type is good)
- Loctite 414
- Parallel-jaw pliers
- Flat, unwaxed fly-tying thread (Kevlar, or the GSP thread used in the following demonstration, is ideal)
- Fly-tying bobbin (if you have one)
- Aquaseal
- Cotol-240 Accelerator (this isn't strictly necessary, but it speeds things up)

STEP 1: Cut away any damaged portion of the fly line and trim both ends so that they are clean and square.

Hold the cut end of one piece of line against a tabletop. Beginning about an inch from the tip, angle the knife blade into the coating of the fly line, cutting downward at a shallow angle toward the tip of the line. When the blade reaches the core of the fly line, turn the blade

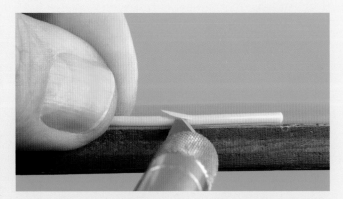

parallel to the tabletop so that you are shaving away the line coating that lies above the core, as shown here. When you reach the tip of the line, angle the blade downward again, and trim the tip to a shallow taper, as shown in the next step.

The idea here is to trim away the coating and expose the line core over the middle ¾ inch or so of the cut. You don't want to damage the core by cutting into it, only to lay bare the top surface of the core. When making this cut, work slowly; it is better to shave off the coating in stages rather than cut too deeply and damage the core.

When you've trimmed the end of one piece of line, make an identical cut, or as close to it as you get, at the end of the other piece of line to be spliced. Certainly straight-angle cuts would be easier to mate, but they expose too little of the fly-line core; as in the needle splice, the glue here must bond together the cores, not the coatings, of the two pieces of line.

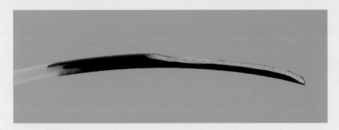

STEP 2: Here's what you're after on the end of each piece of line—a sloping cut at the rear, a straight section of exposed core, and a sloping cut at the tip. The coating of the fly line has been colored black here for better visibility of the cut.

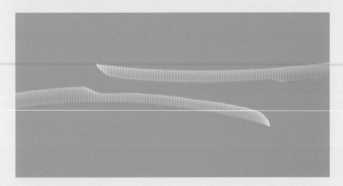

STEP 3: The cut faces on the two pieces of line will be mated and glued. Test-fit the ends of the line to see how well they fit. It's not necessary to get an exact match, but you do want to get the two pieces to mate as cleanly as possible, with no big gaps or unevenness in length. Do any additional trimming that might be necessary to get a good fit.

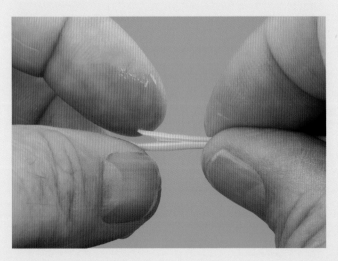

STEP 4: Apply the Loctite to the cut surfaces on both pieces of line, covering both the exposed cores and the tapering portions of the cuts.

At this point, it gets a bit messy, though it isn't too bad. Place the glued surfaces together and press them together with your fingertips. Use your left and right fingertips alternately, working up and down the splice, pinching the glued surfaces into contact. This type of glue gets tacky and begins to adhere when pressure is applied. At first, the pieces of line won't stick together; just continue pinching the glue joint up and down the splice. Some glue will squeeze out and get on your fingertips; to prevent gluing your fingers to the line, keep them moving, working along the splice, pressing and releasing, pressing and releasing. If your fingers begin to stick to the line or stick together, don't pull them straight apart; use a sliding motion, rolling your thumb against your forefinger to peel them away from one another.

Here's a little tip given to me by a hobby store owner who uses this type of glue regularly. After applying the glue, moisten your fingertips—just damp, not dripping wet—as you press the splice together. The moisture helps prevent your fingers from sticking but doesn't interfere with the bond.

STEP 5: After 10 or 15 seconds of applying pressure to the splice, the glue will become tacky and the two pieces of line will begin to stick to one another. Continue pinching and rolling the glued area until a bond is formed all along the splice and you can release the line without the splice coming apart.

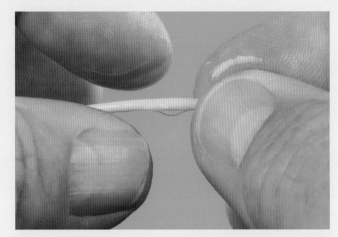

STEP 6: Use the pair of pliers to squeeze the splice lengthwise. Apply firm pressure, but not so much that you flatten the relatively soft coating of the line. Squeeze and hold briefly, then reposition the pliers up and down the splice to apply pressure to all parts of the glue joint and get a good bond. Then rotate the fly line, using the

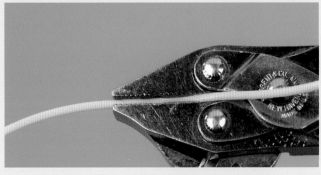

pliers to apply pressure to all sides of the splice and to keep the glued area round in cross section, since even mild pressure from the pliers will deform it slightly. Simply use the pliers to squeeze the line back to shape. If the jaws are serrated, you'll leave some indentations in the line; this is fine.

STEP 7: You may find this hard to believe—I did—but if you let the glue cure for 5 or 10 minutes, you can fish the line as it is. I was deeply skeptical when I first saw this, but

the strength of this splice was repeatedly demonstrated to me. If you have the proper adhesive, you can actually form this splice on the water if necessary and continue fishing.

Eventually, though, the thin tapering tips of the splice will, under repeated flexing, begin to peel up from the joint and snag on the guides as the line slides through. To seal the tips down and make the whole splice smoother and permanent, Buhr takes a few additional steps.

STEP 8: Covering the ends of the splice with thread will seal them down. The easiest way to do this is to mount a spool of thread in a fly-tying bobbin; wrap the thread around one of the bobbin arms to provide some tension. Strip off 6 to 8 inches of thread, and pinch the tag of the thread against the middle of the splice. Then swing the fly line like a jump rope to spin the bobbin around the line, laying down wraps of thread. Guide the position of the wraps with the tips of your thumbs. Wrap the thread down the splice, continuing about ⅛ inch beyond the splice end. Then reverse direction and wrap over the splice and ⅛ inch beyond the other end, stopping as needed to pull more thread from the bobbin.

If you don't have a bobbin, you can make these wraps with a cut length of thread, though it's a little tedious. You don't need a great deal of thread pressure; wraps should be firm, but not so tight that they deform the fly-line coating.

STEP 9: When the thread wraps are complete, tie off the thread with one or two half hitches, and trim it off. Put a thin film of Loctite over the thread wraps. Use a pinching-and-rolling motion with thumb and forefinger to squeeze the glue into the thread; the pressure helps the glue set more quickly. Again, moistening your fingertips will help prevent them from sticking.

The glue will be dry to the touch in just a couple of minutes. The thread wraps have a rough surface, and to smooth them out you can coat them with Aquaseal, using exactly the procedure shown on page 99. Again, the use of an accelerator is recommended to shorten the curing time and reduce the amount of tending that is required to keep the Aquaseal from sagging. Here's the finished splice coated with Aquaseal.

FIELD FIXES

Damage to fly lines is rarely so severe as to require onstream, on-the-spot repair. In most cases, you can limp through the day with a damaged line; it may pose an inconvenience, but you can stay fishing. And provided you have the supplies, most repairs of the type noted above can be performed back at camp or at the lodge; packing Cotol-240 Accelerator in your field repair kit makes overnight repairs possible.

SLEEVE SPLICE

In extreme cases, if a fly line is cut completely in half or the core is badly abraded, the damage will need immediate attention. Fortunately, if you come prepared, a sleeve splice can be rather simply performed. It's not much to look at, and you'll feel it and hear it on every cast, but it is strong and will keep you fishing.

STEP 1: Cut away any damage on the line until you have two clean ends for the splice. For the repair, you'll need a 4- to 6-inch length of braided monofilament, shown at the top. This material is available at some fly shops for making leaders or line/leader connectors. (Dacron fly-line backing, trolling line, or squidding line can also be used, and in fact is superior in one respect: It stretches less than nylon. But it can be difficult to locate a di-

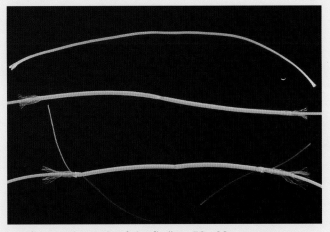

ameter of braided Dacron large enough to fit over the ends of the fly line; 50-, 80-, or even 100-pound line may be required.) You'll also need about 18 inches of ordinary 12- to 15-pound monofilament.

Insert the cut ends of the fly line inside the ends of the mono braid, as shown in the middle. The ends of the fly line should meet at the middle of the braid.

Then use the monofilament to tie a nail knot at each end of the braid; cinch them tightly, as shown at the bottom. Trim the mono tags and any frayed braid. That's it. This repair is actually strong enough to be permanent, and if you wish, you can coat the knots with a thin film of Aquaseal to smooth over the roughness and make them slide better through the guides.

CHAPTER FOUR

WADERS

A SMASHED ROD OR A MALFUNCTIONING REEL can, under the worst of circumstances, prove a trip-ending catastrophe; at the very least, it'll send your day downhill pretty fast. Happily, however, these things don't happen too often. Leaky waders, on the other hand, are less dramatic but far more common, the kind of small-scale annoyance that can drive you nuts over the course of a day or season. Wader leaks get my vote for the single most irritating equipment-related problem in fly fishing for the simple reason that they involve personal comfort. In one respect, waders are a bit like fly lines—materials and construction give them an intrinsically limited life span, though they rarely come to a sudden end. Performance just slowly declines, one aggravating leak at a time.

Fortunately, waders are, at least in many cases, one of the easiest types of equipment to repair, and the prospect for an extended lifetime is good. But as always, one of the best ways to ensure long service from your waders is to eliminate, or at least minimize, preventable damage that comes from improper use, care, or storage. Far more wader leaks are traceable to these causes than is commonly supposed; we only notice leaks when we're on the water and sometimes fail to draw the connection between a wet pant leg and prior treatment of the equipment.

PREVENTION

- Though it may seem obvious, buy waders that fit. If the inseam is too short, walking and wading put unnecessary stress on seams in the crotch; if the legs are too long, excess fabric can chafe and abrade. Wearing stockingfoot waders with overly small booties stresses the foot seams.

  Wader legs and uppers should fit to give you good mobility. When trying on a pair of waders, test-fit them by crouching into a deep-knee bend. When you squat, you should feel no tugging or binding at the knees or seat; when you stand up, the waders shouldn't be excessively baggy in the knees or legs.

If you're on the borderline between two sizes, get the larger one, especially if you fish in cool or cold weather and will be wearing bulky clothing underneath.

- By the same token, buy properly sized boots for stockingfoot waders. Boots that are too large allow your feet to slip inside and chafe the bootie material. Overly tight boots can stress bootie seams as you force your foot inside the boot. When buying boots, it's best to bring along your waders, the type of socks you typically wear under them, and any oversocks that you intend to wear over the wader booties. Put them all on when you test-fit new boots.

- Put stockingfoots on properly. Grabbing the wader leg and forcing your foot down into a snug bootie strains the foot seams and those joining the booties to the upper portion of the wader. Instead, bunch up the leg fabric in your hands until you reach the top of the bootie; slide your toes in, and then grab the back of the bootie and pull it over your heel. Think of donning your waders less like putting on a pair of pants and more like putting on a pair of socks.

- Once your stockingfoot waders are on, don't stand or walk around on dirt, sand, gravel, or asphalt. Aside from the obvious risk of an outright puncture, the nylon facing on the neoprene booties will pick up tiny particles of grit. They may be small, but they are sharp and irregularly shaped, like broken glass. Under the pressure of walking and wading, the particles can eventually migrate through the neoprene and cause a seep or pinhole leak. When putting on or taking off your waders, stand on a reasonably dirt-free surface—the floor mat of a car, a square of indoor/outdoor carpeting carried for the purpose, or even a gear bag. From time to time, hose off the mat or carpeting to prevent grit from accumulating.

- For the same reason, wear gravel guards. Sand and dirt can easily enter exposed boot tops, work their way into the feet, and abrade the booties as you walk or wade.

- When fishing where abrasive materials are particularly likely to find their way inside wading boots, take an extra precaution. Some striper fishermen, for instance, who wade beaches where wave action continually washes sand over and around wading boots, wear a pair of thick socks over the booties to help protect the neoprene. One wader expert told me that he thinks all saltwater anglers should wear an extra pair of neoprene socks over their wader booties. Wading boots, of course, must be sized to accommodate the extra bulk, but the extra socks will add significantly to the life of the booties by protecting them from abrasion and reducing sole compression.

- If you routinely fish from a kneeling position, consider wearing knee pads of the type used by basketball players or gardeners. They prevent wear and abrasion, and they're significantly more comfortably than kneeling down without any protection. You can instead wear a separate pair of gravel guards over your knees, or in a pinch, even pull your regular gravel guards up to cover your knees.

- No one wants to let the tail wag the dog and let concerns about waders dictate where you can or can't fish. At the same time, however, a bit of common sense goes a long way. If you habitually hike or bushwack through thick country, consider an extra layer of protection. Thorny vegetation, broken limbs and stobs on deadfalls, and barbed wire can take their toll, and a pair of brush chaps or thick rain pants can help ward off punctures and be removed when you reach the water.

- Rope-sling driftboat seats or rough wooden ones can also be tough on waders. Though punctures may not be a problem, these coarse surfaces can work to loosen the waterproofing seam tape on the seat of the waders, particularly if you are rowing. Sit on a boat cushion, towel, or even a jacket to reduce the abrasion.

- Avoid subjecting your waders to extreme temperatures for prolonged periods of time. Keeping them in a car trunk during the summer, for instance, can dry out the neoprene and shorten its life.

- To be on the safe side, don't let breathable waders come into contact with gasoline, motor oil, heavy doses of sunscreen, or insect repellent containing DEET. While the exterior fabric on most waders is impervious to these chemicals, a breathable membrane, if it is exposed anywhere, can be attacked and damaged by them, especially DEET.

- When you're finished fishing and return home or to camp or to a lodge, unpack your waders and let them dry. If you're using them daily, simply hang them up or drape them over a clothesline or fence rail—anything to get them up off the ground and let air circulate. When you're finished for the season, see the "Storage" section below.

CARE AND MAINTENANCE

Waders do not require a great deal of maintenance or upkeep, but they do need some, particularly the stockingfoot type, since the booties are a high-wear area vulnerable to abrasion. As with virtually all fly tackle, dirt is the enemy.

CLEANING

Just as you should take care to keep stockingfoot booties free of dirt when you put on your waders, so you should make an effort to keep them clean when you're through for the day. Even if you wear gravel guards, some amount of dirt or sand will inevitably find its way inside your boots. Before packing up after a day on the water, it's good practice to rinse the feet of your stockingfoots in the stream or lake you've been fishing, rubbing away any accumulations of mud or silt. Dirt is easier to remove when the waders are still wet; once it dries and cakes, it's more trouble to get off.

If an immediate rinsing is impractical, hose off or rinse the wader feet when you return home, using a soft brush or rag to loosen any surface dirt that won't readily wash free. Hosing off the uppers as well certainly doesn't hurt, but because this part of the wader is often subject to repeated wetting and drying during the day, the dirt tends to adhere more firmly and a simple rinsing isn't always effective in removing it. If, however, the waders have been used in salt water, hose off the entire exterior to remove as much salt residue as possible. Give extra attention to metal components such as suspender buttons or pocket zippers that might corrode. After rinsing, onstream or at home, hang the waders up to dry.

Even waders that have been rinsed regularly after use should, from time to time, be cleaned more thoroughly—that is, washed. How often depends upon the frequency of use and the material from which the wader is constructed. But I find that, at least under ordinary conditions, once a season or so is sufficient. Aside from eliminating that swamplike aroma that well-used waders sometime acquire, washing also removes more deeply embedded grit from booties, knees, seat, and other areas where dirt can be ground into the wader fabric.

Washing breathable waders, however, not only promotes durability but also improves performance as well. Breathable waders employ a microporous coating or membrane that contains tiny holes, small enough to prevent liquid water from entering but large enough to let water vapor from your body escape. This breathable material in the wader is never on the outside; it is either on the inside or, more often, sandwiched between the interior and exterior fabrics. Water vapor, then, must pass not only through the breathable coating or membrane, but also through at least one, and often two, layers of fabric. If the surface of the fabric is contaminated—with dirt, algae, minerals from salt water or other materials that dry on the exterior of the wader, or by salt or oils from perspiration on the inside—the transmission of water vapor is hindered. The waders remain waterproof, but breathability declines. Water condenses more readily on the inside of the waders, and you end up with that sticky, clammy feel. When it comes to breathable waders, the cleaner the better.

The procedure for washing waders varies with the style, material, and manufacturer. All bootfoot-style waders and all waders made entirely of neoprene should be washed by hand. Any breathable wader can be washed by hand, but some—Orvis breathable waders, for instance—are machine washable. Be certain to consult the manufacturer's instructions, as machine washing some waders may damage them. Never dry-clean any wader, and never use bleach or detergents containing additives such as whiteners. A plain, powdered detergent with no additives is fine. Ivory Snow powder, for instance, is excellent for the purpose.

Handwashing goes just as you'd expect—in a bathtub or basin of soapy water, warm or cold depending on the manufacturer's instructions, but never hot. I let my waders soak for a while, sometimes several hours, to loosen the dirt. Then just grab a handful of fabric in each hand and go to it, scrubbing them against one another and gradually working your way over the entire surface of the waders. On extremely dirty areas, such as the knees, I use a soft brush to do a more thorough job. Most of the time, the overall scrubbing and agitation of the waders washes both the inside and outside simultaneously. But if the inside of the waders is particularly in need of cleaning (a common problem with neoprene, which doesn't breathe), you can turn them inside out and wash the interior fabric.

After washing, rinse the waders. Rinsing under a running tap is a bit laborious; I find it easier to do the job under a showerhead or outside with a hose. Rinse the waders; turn them inside out, and rinse again. Then dry them as explained below.

If you're machine washing your waders, follow the manufacturer's instructions, using warm or cold water as indicated. I wash on a gentle cycle just to be safe. When the waders are clean, air-dry them; never put waders in a clothes dryer.

DRYING

Whether they've just come back from a fishing trip or just come out of the wash, waders should be dried. Rolling them up or stuffing them in a wader bag when they're wet encourages mold or mildew; in addition, metal components such as suspender buttons can rust or corrode, and prolonged dampness may damage some materials used in the suspenders.

To air-dry stockingfoot waders, simply hang them—full length, if possible—in a warm, dry place. Given enough time, the waders will dry inside and out. But you can speed things up (especially with neoprene stockingfoot waders) by turning them inside out after the exterior surface is dry.

Drying bootfoot waders requires more time; the materials used in constructing the soles, and sometimes the boots themselves, take longer to dry. You can hasten the process by taking out any removable insoles to dry separately. Then roll or fold the waders down to the tops of the boot feet to get better air circulation inside the boots. Even then, drying can take a while, and some anglers stuff loosely crumpled sheets of newspaper inside the boots, right down to the toe, to absorb moisture.

And to some extent this does help. Other anglers use a fan, a hair dryer (low heat), or a vacuum cleaner with the hose reversed to blow air into the boots and speed up evaporation. There are even commercially available boot dryers that will do the job. But the upshot is that drying bootfoots takes some time, so it's best to wash them when you won't be needing them for a while.

STORAGE

To store waders for a short time—between trips, for instance—you can either hang them up or, if they are thoroughly dry, roll them up and pack them in a wader bag, ready for use. To store them for a longer time, such as between seasons, it's better to hang them or fold them loosely. A tight fold can produce sharp creases that weaken the material. You can hang waders by the suspenders, but elastic suspenders can fatigue and stretch over time. I prefer to clip the wader tops to a wire coat hanger using clothespins. Wire hangers usually aren't strong enough to support bootfoot waders; in that case, I wedge the boot feet into the frame of a wooden clothes hanger and hang the waders upside down. And if you have the space, any pair of waders can be stored flat—under a bed, for example, or in an attic. Waders in longer-term storage should be kept away from heat and direct sunlight, preferably where the air is not excessively damp, and away from electric motors, which produce ozone.

RESTORING WATER REPELLENCY

On breathable waders, the exterior fabric is treated with a durable water repellent (DWR). This finish treatment has nothing to do with the actual waterproofness of the waders; rather, the DWR causes water on the outside of the waders to bead up and roll off. Without such a treatment, the waders themselves would remain waterproof, but the exterior fabric of the waders would absorb water, making them heavier, less comfortable, and less breathable. And the waders would take a longer time to dry after fishing.

Since the DWR is applied to the exterior fabric, it wears off from constant exposure to sunlight and water and eventually needs to be restored if you wish to get the best performance from your waders. The loss of water repellency is gradual, and depending on wader use, can take two or three seasons, maybe more. When water no longer beads up and rolls off the waders, and parts of the fabric—typically the wader legs—begin to absorb water, it's probably time to re-treat them.

Restoring the DWR requires a product formulated specifically for the purpose; ReviveX and Nikwax are popular types. Such treatments are often available in two versions. One type is applied by putting it in a washing machine with the waders; it gives good coverage of the fabric and is convenient to use. A second type is sprayed directly onto the waders. It's not difficult to apply—just follow the directions on the label—and it's your only option if the wader manufacturer recommends against putting your waders in a washing machine. In both cases, however, the waders must be clean prior to applying the treatment or the surface treatment may not adhere well.

CHECKUP

There's little need to check waders for leaks; they will announce themselves all on their own. But periodically inspecting the waders can alert you to potential problems before they develop into leaks.

Take a close look at the wader seams, and specifically the seam tape used to protect and reinforce the seam; in breathable waders, this tape keeps the seam waterproof. The tape is secured with a heat-activated glue; it can work loose and cause a leak.

Turn the waders inside out. Beginning at one end of a seam, follow it along, looking for any place that the tape has rippled, peeled, loosened, or separated altogether from the fabric. Mark these areas with a felt pen or piece of duct tape for repair later, as shown on page 131. Most breathable waders are taped only on the inside, but some neoprene waders are taped on both the inside and the outside, in which case turn the waders right-side out and inspect the exterior seams. Pay special attention to seam tape on the seat and the feet, areas particularly prone to chafing. If you sit in a driftboat or raft all day, shifting your weight, turning or sliding, it's possible, over time, to peel up an edge of the seam tape and work the tape free. Anglers who fish a lot from float tubes often have this same problem, since kicking with fins tends to rub and chafe seam tape on the wader seat. Bootie seams on stockingfoots, both inside and out, tend to rub against socks or wading boots, and the tape can loosen.

When inspecting seams at the crotch and inseam of breathable waders, be alert for signs of abrasion or wear at the edge of the seam tape. The taped seam is stiffer than the surrounding fabric, and the edge of the tape becomes a hinge point when the fabric is flexed. The fabric will fold or crease along the edge of the tape, producing a "corner" that is subject to chafing. If you see any fraying or abrasion on the exterior fabric at the tape edges, mark it for repair and attend to it before the abrasion becomes a leak.

Neoprene booties on breathable stockingfoot waders, and the surface of any wader made entirely of neoprene, are worth examining as well.

The neoprene itself is actually sandwiched between two thin facings of knit fabric. Sometimes you can detect the beginnings of a leak where the facing fabric on the outside is cut or abraded and you can see the rubberlike neoprene beneath, as shown here. There may be no leak yet, but it is a weak spot worth reinforcing as explained below. If you find such a spot, circle it with a felt-tipped pen or apply a piece of duct tape to mark the spot for repair.

REPAIR

The vast majority of wader leaks are punctures in the fabric (as opposed to seam leaks, which are explained below), and in most cases, these can be successfully repaired. It's useful, however, to consider wader repair in the same light as cleaning and lubricating reels—manufacturers' instructions vary somewhat in their particulars, and it's always prudent to abide by the specific recommendations concerning products, procedures, and even the types of repair that are advisable. Some manufacturers, for instance, discourage seam repairs to the point where attempting them can void the warranty. Still, there is substantial overlap in the repair techniques, and these are explained in the sections that follow.

Before you can fix a leak, however, you must find it. Visible tears, cuts, and larger punctures, of course, are obvious. The problem arises with tiny punctures and pinhole leaks that are difficult or impossible to see, particularly in neoprene. When neoprene is punctured, the elasticity of the material causes it to contract around the hole, making the puncture virtually invisible. The hole will still leak; you just can't see it. To a lesser extent, the same thing is true of breathable waders; the weave of the exterior fabric, separated by a small puncture, will close up, leaving little evidence of a hole. Generally, finding pinhole leaks is the biggest problem in repairing them.

FINDING PINHOLES

There are four basic approaches to finding pinhole leaks. Three of them are suitable for any type of wader—neoprene or breathable—but if you have a leak in the breathable portion of your waders, you may want to go directly to the fourth technique, the alcohol method, which is fairly simple and usually gives good results. This method, however, does not work with neoprene waders or booties. All of these techniques do require that you have at least a general sense of where the leak is—in the right foot, for example, or behind the left knee. The more narrowly you can localize the area of the leak, the more quickly you can find its exact location.

FLASHLIGHT METHOD. The flashlight method is quite simple, and because the waders remain dry, it's not as potentially messy as other approaches. The downside is that it's not always possible to locate a leak this way; very small pinholes can elude detection.

You'll need a strong flashlight, preferably one with a big, wide lens; little "key chain" flashlights are tedious to use and don't give good results. You'll also need a permanent marker. Turn your waders inside out and, in a completely dark room, put the flashlight inside them. Pull the wader fabric in the general area of the leak smooth and taut over the flashlight lens. The pinhole leak will show as a bright spot coming through the fabric. If you don't see a bright spot, move the flashlight around, inspecting new portions of the fabric until you locate the leak. Then use the marker to draw a small circle around it.

INFLATION METHOD. This method works well, but it is a bit more involved. It requires a vacuum cleaner that can be configured to blow air—usually a canister type in which the hose can be plugged into the vacuum exhaust—and this method really works better with two people. You also need a solution of one part dishwashing liquid to three parts water; a pint or so is ample.

Bunch the top of the waders around the vacuum-cleaner hose and hold them tightly. Switch on the vacuum to inflate the waders. To locate the leak, you want to maintain enough pressure inside the waders to force air through the puncture, but not so much that you put unnecessary stress on the wader seams. This is where another person comes in handy. After the waders are inflated, your partner can seal and hold them very tightly around the hose to minimize air escape, turning the vacuum on and off as needed to maintain pressure. Or the wader tops can be loosened to provide an escape valve, and the vacuum simply left running.

Once the waders are inflated, use a rag or sponge to wipe some soap solution over the suspected area, and watch for small soap bubbles formed by escaping air to appear on the surface of the fabric. If the waders aren't too wet, you can usually circle the leak with a marker, at least enough to find the leak for repair when the waders dry. Or you can pinch the fabric at the puncture, turn the waders inside out, and mark the leak as closely as you can on the dry side.

Another approach to inflating waders for the purpose of detecting leaks is shown in the section on "Field Fixes" since the method requires no equipment and is suitable for use on the water or when traveling.

WATER METHOD. The water method is the messiest of all and, again, generally works best with two people. I consider it a last resort, but occasionally it seems to be the only way to locate a leak, particularly in neoprene waders or booties. And in fact, the method is really best suited to locating leaks in the feet or lower legs. But it must be done carefully to avoid stressing wader seams.

Turn the waders inside out. In a bathtub or outdoors, pour some water into the leg of the wader where the leak is suspected. How much water is the question; you need enough volume so that the pressure forces water through the leak, but not so much that the wader seams are stressed. A couple of gallons is usually enough. If the leak is, say, in the foot, examine the bootie of the wader carefully. For a pinhole leak, don't expect to see a gusher of water squirting through the waders; you'll probably just see a few beads of water forming on the wader fabric or perhaps a small dribble coming through. Circle the hole with a marker. If you don't see a leak, and you're certain that the water level is above the puncture, hold the waders closed tightly above the water level, and gently squeeze the water-filled portion to increase the pressure and force water through the puncture. Squeezing too hard, however, can cause additional damage.

If the leak is above the foot area—say, in the knee—you'll need to lift up both ends of the waders so that the water collects in the suspected area of the leak. Again, you can squeeze gently to increase the pressure.

Under no circumstances should you ever (a) fill the waders with water; the cumulative pressure can force water through a seam, particularly in the feet, and you end up with a much bigger problem than you started with; or (b) suspend the waders from a showerhead to put water in (a temptation if you are working alone). Remember that a gallon of water weighs 8 pounds. I've heard more than one story of plumbing being damaged this way.

ALCOHOL METHOD. This method is suitable only for breathable fabric, but it usually works pretty well. Fill a small spray bottle with rubbing alcohol. Saturate the exterior of the wader over the suspected area of the leak. Immediately turn the waders inside out. Molecules of alcohol are much smaller than those of water. They will readily migrate through the puncture and be absorbed by the fabric on the interior of the wader. Look for a dark spot to appear on the lining of the wader; the puncture is at or very near the center of the spot. Circle it with a marker.

FINDING COMPRESSION AND ABRASION LEAKS

The neoprene feet or booties of waders can suffer from compression leaks. The neoprene used in waders is not a solid material, but rather contains tiny bubbles encased in a matrix of synthetic rubber. If the material is repeatedly compressed and the pressure is maintained, over time the bubbles can rupture and provide an entry point for water. Or the material becomes thin with sustained compression and more susceptible to punctures.

Compression leaks most often occur in the heel of the bootie from the force of standing and walking. If you're using the water method to locate the damage, a compression leak will appear as a damp spot on the bootie sole as water seeps through many small channels simultaneously in an area that may be as large as an inch or more in diameter. If you're using the inflation method, you'll see a patch of small bubbles on the surface of the material. Use a waterproof marker to draw a generously sized circle around the damage.

Like compression leaks, abrasion leaks occur over an area of the wader rather than in a small, localized spot. Routinely kneeling to fish without protecting the waders, for instance, can eventually abrade the knees to the point where water seeps in. Larger areas like this can be patched as explained below.

FINDING SEAM LEAKS

Breathable waders are constructed by stitching pieces of fabric together, and the sewing itself does not make the seam waterproof. The waterproof barrier is provided by the seam tape that covers the joined material and stitch holes. A seam leak in breathable waders means that the tape has failed somewhere; it has separated from the fabric, in a way that may be obvious or not, allowing water to seep through. Strictly speaking, repairing such a leak is really a repair to the seam tape rather than the seam itself.

Seam leaks are sometimes easy to detect, sometimes not. I've had mixed results finding seam leaks using the alcohol method, but because the method is simple, I usually try it first. I've had better luck with the water or inflation methods. The leak will appear somewhere at the edge of the seam tape. The procedures for repairing it are explained below.

Neoprene waders and booties on breathables are usually constructed by butt-gluing pieces of neoprene, sometimes in conjunction with blind-stitching, a sewing technique that does not put stitch holes completely through the fabric. But the glue itself makes the seam waterproof, though the seam is usually finished with waterproof tape as well. This type of construction has two consequences. First, in some cases if a seam is breached, water can migrate underneath the tape until it finds an exit hole; you can find this hole using the water or inflation methods, but it may not be located exactly at the spot of the actual seam separation. Second, you may be able to repair the actual seam damage rather than just patching the exit hole in the tape. This method is explained below.

After a leak of any type has been located, you have several repair options, depending on the wader material, the manufacturer, the location of the leak, and the extent of the damage.

IRON-ON PATCHES

A few manufacturers, Orvis among them, recommend iron-on tape and patch material and supply it with their waders. Note that this is not the same as the iron-on patches or binding tape that you might find at a fabric store; those materials are generally not waterproof and won't make a watertight repair. The virtues of an iron-on repair are simplicity and speed; the patching requires no glue and hence no drying time. Iron-on patches, however, are only suitable for breathable wader material—not neoprene. This type of repair should be performed on the inside surface of the waders, where these patches give better adhesion.

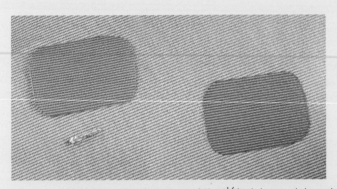

Small punctures, rips, or tears, such as the one pictured at the lower left, can be repaired with a single strip of iron-on patch. Turn on an iron to a low-steam, polyester/rayon setting and let it heat. Turn the waders inside out; clean the repair area thoroughly with rubbing alcohol, and let it dry.

Cut a piece of iron-on patch material large enough to extend ⅛ to ¼ inch beyond the edges of the damaged area, as shown at the upper left. This overlap is important for adhesion of the tape; if the damage is so large or irregularly shaped that it doesn't allow for this excess margin of patch material, you'll have to use one of the patching methods described below. I like to round the corners of the patch to prevent them from snagging or catching and reduce the risk that they will peel up.

Smooth the waders over an ironing board so that there are no wrinkles or creases beneath the patching area. If the edges of the damage are raised up or curled, flatten them as much as possible. You can iron them gently to smooth them out and prevent any fabric from bunching up beneath the tape. Position the patch over the leak, taking note in the manufacturer's instructions of which side of the patch is placed against the wader fabric. Press the iron on top of the patch and hold it there for about ten seconds. Make sure that the iron covers all the edges of the patch; you want to get a good seal around the perimeter. Remove the heat, and rub the surface of the patch back and forth with a second piece of fabric until the repair has cooled, as shown at the right.

Larger tears can be mended with more than one piece of tape provided the damage is such that the patch overlaps the edges sufficiently to give plenty of contact surface with the wader fabric.

The L-shaped tear at the left, for instance, can be patched with two pieces of tape, shown here flanking the damage. Again, round the corners of the tape.

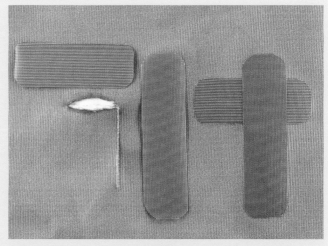

The completed repair is shown at the right. Note that the second piece of tape completely overlaps the end of the first and is secured against the wader fabric. When performing this type of repair, press an edge of the iron against the edges where the top piece of tape crosses the bottom one; you want to get a secure, waterproof bond at the overlap.

When applying longer strips of tape, avoid the temptation to work the iron back and forth over the surface of the tape, as you might iron a piece of clothing. Once the tape adhesive liquefies from the heat, pressure from the iron can wrinkle or bunch the tape or shift it out of position, at which point glue may be transferred to the iron.

A rip or tear too large or irregular in shape to be covered with an iron-on patch can be repaired by using the iron-on material to affix a separate piece of fabric over the damage. This repair fabric is not itself an iron-on patch, but is essentially a piece of waterproof material similar to that from which the wader is made. A swatch of this fabric may be supplied when you purchase the waders, or is available in a separate repair kit. Or if you have an old pair of breathable waders that have given up the ghost, it's always worth cutting out and saving a few pieces of fabric from somewhere near the top of the waders on the back, since this area sees less wear and the material here is likely to be in good condition. Clean the material thoroughly and save it for use as patches.

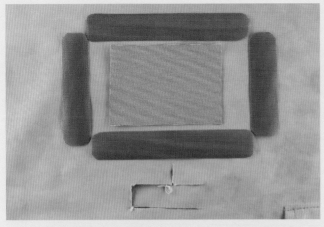

STEP 1: To patch a large tear, shown at the bottom of the photo, cut a piece of repair fabric large enough to fit comfortably over the repair area, as shown at the top. Cut the edges of the patch as straight as you can get them; a curved or wandering edge can be difficult to secure with a straight length of tape.

Cut strips of repair tape long enough to secure edge of the patch and round the edges, as shown. In this type of repair, I like to make sure that the edges of the tape overlap to form the shape of the number sign (#). This ensures that the very ends of the tape are bonded to the wader fabric itself, as shown in the next step.

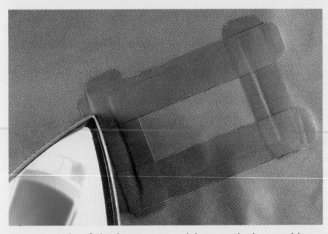

STEP 2: Turn the waders inside out and lay them flat on an ironing board. Make sure that the surface of the waders to which the tape will be applied is clean.

With your hands or a warm iron, smooth the edges of the damage flat. Place the patch over the damaged area, and use iron-on tape or strips of iron-patch material to bond the edges of the patch fabric to the waders using the method explained above. As you apply each strip of the iron-on material, smooth the patching material out so that there are no folds, wrinkles, or creases at the edge. And as noted above, press the edge of iron into the "ledges" formed where one strip of iron-on material crosses another, as shown here, to get a tight bond.

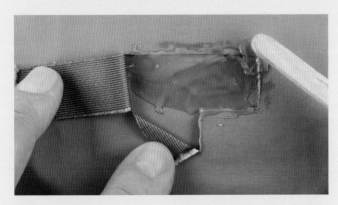

STEP 3: Turn the waders right-side out. If there is a loose edge or flap of material, as shown here, it should be glued down to prevent it from snagging on brush or other obstructions and tearing further. You can glue it down with Aquaseal (see "Glue Repairs" for details about this adhesive).

First, work some Aquaseal under the loose edges of the material.

STEP 4: Smooth the loose edges against the surface of the patch, getting them to lie as flat as possible. Then apply a film of Aquaseal over the torn edges, using a moistened finger as explained on page 126 to smooth out the adhesive.

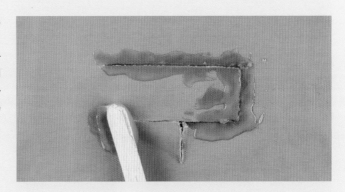

GLUE REPAIRS

Using an adhesive—either by itself or to secure a piece of patching material—is by far the most common approach to mending waders. Anglers use various types of glue, but probably the most popular and certainly the one most often recommended by wader manufacturers is Aquaseal. It is widely available, has good adhesion, is fairly simple to use, is strong and durable, and maintains flexibility when dry. When you're finished using Aquaseal, wipe clean the threads on the tube and cap, and close tightly. Aquaseal can, over time, dry in the tube, and the best place for long-term storage is in the freezer.

The downside to Aquaseal is that it requires 10 to 12 hours to dry and 24 hours to cure fully. For an off-season repair, the drying time may be of little consequence; on a trip, however, it may mean a full day's fishing time spent waiting for your waders to dry. You can hasten the process significantly by using Cotol-240 Cure Accelerator, a product of the McNett Corporation, which also manufactures Aquaseal. Cotol will decrease the drying time down to about two hours. The accelerator is mixed with the adhesive—usually one part accelerator to three or four parts Aquaseal—prior to applying the glue to the waders. Mix them together with a toothpick or a clean stick or even a knife blade on a piece of aluminum foil or plastic lid.

In fact, Cotol is so useful that I rarely use Aquaseal without it—whether in mending waders or for other uses described in this book. And I always pack Cotol in my field kit to avoid long, repair-related downtime on a fishing trip.

Though Aquaseal can be applied to either the inside or outside of breathable waders, most manufacturers recommend that it be used on the interior surface; typically, the inside fabric offers better adhesion. In some cases, however, you have no choice but to apply it to the exterior. Either way, the fabric surface should be as clean and dry as possible. On repairs I'm performing at home, I wash the damaged area with soap, water, and a stiff brush to remove dirt that may be embedded in the weave of the fabric. When the waders are dry, I wipe the area with alcohol or Cotol to remove any remaining contaminants. Neoprene waders can be patched on the inside, outside, or both.

GLUE-ONLY REPAIRS

Many types of leaks, particularly pinhole leaks and small punctures, can be mended using Aquaseal alone without a separate piece of patching fabric.

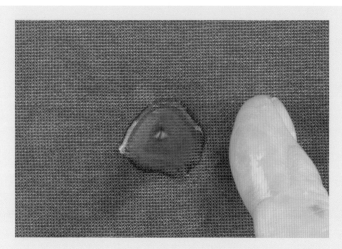

After locating the leak, simply smear a dab of Aquaseal over the site. (If you are using the alcohol method to locate a pinhole leak in breathable waders, you don't need to wait for the alcohol to dry.) After applying the adhesive, moisten your index finger with water and lightly rub the surface of the patch back and forth to smooth out any bumps or irregularities that might rub on your clothing. Keep the patch level until it is dry.

For glue-only repairs to neoprene waders, I take a slightly different approach.

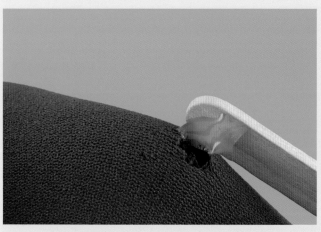

If the waders are wet after locating the leak, let them dry completely. Then put your hand on the fabric behind the damage. Push on the hole from behind with your fingertip to stretch the neoprene and open the hole slightly, as shown here. With your finger or an applicator, force some glue down into the hole, as much and as deeply as you can. Relax pressure on the hole, and let the neoprene contract around the adhesive. Then apply and smooth another dab of Aquaseal over the surface of the waders, as shown in the previous photo.

When the patch is dry, I usually turn the waders inside out and repair the other side of the hole in exactly the same way, just for insurance.

There is another repair that, strictly speaking, is a glue-only type, but it does require that you have a special kind of tape that is employed temporarily in the repair process. Because this technique produces a patch that allows the waders to be used almost immediately, it is explained in the "Field Fixes" section at the end of this chapter, but of course, the same repair can be performed at home.

GLUED PATCHES

An alternative to iron-on patches, and a method commonly recommended by manufacturers that do not advise iron-on patching, involves gluing a piece of repair material over the leak. Though this method can certainly be used for pinhole leaks or small rips, it is particularly useful for larger tears or more extensive damage because it reinforces the wader fabric. It is suitable for both breathable waders and neoprenes.

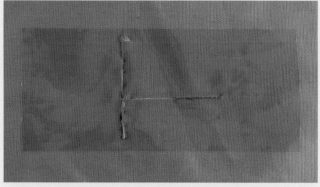

STEP 1: In this method, you must apply glue directly over the damaged area. If the hole or tear is large, it's entirely possible that some adhesive will find its way through the hole or between the edges of the rip and onto the wader fabric underneath it. Without some precautions, you can end up gluing the back and front sides of the waders together. To avoid this unhappy result, you should work against a backing surface of some sort. You can apply a piece of clear cellophane packing tape over the damaged area on the outside of the wader, as shown here, to stop the glue from coming through. Or you can turn the waders inside out and slip a folded newspaper covered with waxed paper behind the repair area. Just about anything that will form a barrier to the glue—without sticking to it—will work.

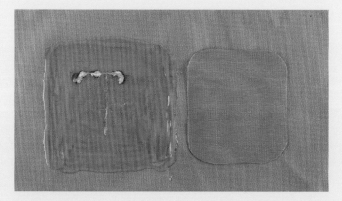

STEP 2: Once the tape is applied, turn the waders inside out. Smooth them out on a flat surface so that there are no wrinkles or folds beneath the repair area. Apply a thin film of Aquaseal over the hole or tear, spreading it at least ½ inch beyond all edges of the damage onto the surrounding wader fabric, as shown at the left. Cut a piece of patching material slightly smaller

than the glued area, as shown at the right, and round the edges. If using patching material supplied with the waders, check to see if it has a paper backing; the backing covers a tacky adhesive on the side of the patch that is to be placed against the glue.

Some manufacturers supply a nonadhesive patch material, and you can also use a patch cut from an old pair of breathable waders, a piece of plain light nylon fabric, or even nylon stocking material. Since the glue itself forms a watertight seal, the patching material need not be waterproof.

STEP 3: Let the Aquaseal get tacky (it takes about five minutes), and press the patch onto the glued area. Smooth the patch with your fingers, working from the center toward the edges, making sure that the fabric lies flat against the waders with no bubbles or wrinkles, and that the edges of the patch are firmly in contact with the adhesive. Keep the patch level until it is dry.

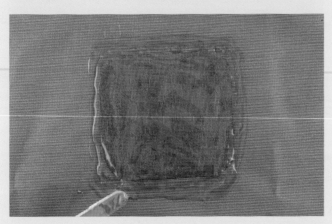

STEP 4: When the adhesive is dry, you can apply a second film of Aquaseal over the entire surface of the patch, essentially sandwiching the fabric patch between two layers of adhesive, as shown here. Use a moistened finger to smooth the surface of the Aquaseal film. Again, keep the patch level. If you've used a tape backing on the exterior of the waders, remove it when the glue is dry.

The same patching technique can be used on neoprene waders, in which case when applying the glue, you want to work some glue into the hole or rip to fill any voids and get adhesive on the torn edges of the neoprene. Neoprene waders can be patched on the inside or the outside. If the damaged area is large or in a high-wear area—seat, crotch, knees, and especially the feet (including neoprene booties on breathable waders)—I like to patch both sides of the wader since I believe this adds durability to the repair. When patching both sides, however, let one patch dry completely before applying the second. Turning your waders inside out when the adhesive is not yet cured may wrinkle or peel off the first patch or even glue the waders together.

COMPRESSION AND ABRASION LEAKS

Compression leaks, as noted earlier, typically occur in the sole of a bootie, particularly in the heel area. They can be repaired by smearing a film of Aquaseal over the damaged area. I usually patch a compression leak on both the inside and the outside of the bootie. You can, if you wish, use a reinforcing patch of separate material as explained above, though sometimes wader booties become curved on the bottom over time, and getting a fabric patch to lie flat against the neoprene can be difficult.

Whether you use a separate fabric patch or not, there are two keys to the repair. First, apply the Aquaseal liberally. Start with a thin film, pressing firmly in a circular motion to work the adhesive into the knit facing fabric on the neoprene; then add additional layers to build up the patch so that the repair forms a smooth surface over the wader fabric. Moisten your finger and rub lightly over the final layer to get it as smooth as possible.

Second, extend the glue patch well beyond the damaged area that you discovered in leak-testing the waders. My experience has been that the actual damage can extend beyond the area that showed leakage in testing, and good coverage will ensure that your foot stays dry.

Abrasion that appears along the edge of the seam tape on breathable waders—usually in the crotch or the inseam—should be repaired, even if it's not yet leaking. Simply apply Aquaseal over the abraded area, forming a thin film that extends about ¼ inch outward on either side of the damage and as far along the seam as the abrasion occurs.

Abrasion leaks on the knees of the waders are best mended with a separate fabric patch, as described on page 127, applied on the outside of the waders. Extra fabric applied on the exterior better protects against further abrasion than a patch on the inside. On breathable waders, there may be one complication. Many breathable waders are made with articulated knees; that is, the legs are constructed in such a way that there is a slight, built-in bend at the knee. It's difficult to get a single, large piece of patching fabric to lie flat against this curved surface. In this case, use separate strips of patching fabric, each about 1 inch wide, glued crosswise, one below the other, over the knee area. It isn't necessary to let one patch dry before applying the next.

SEAM LEAKS

Seam leaks can be the devil's own business—so much so that some manufacturers recommend (or require) that seam leaks be factory repaired, and it's always best to check your wader warranty to see where the manufacturer stands on the issue. But most seam leaks, particularly smaller ones, can be repaired at home, though the techniques vary a bit depending on the material.

BREATHABLE WADERS. As explained previously, seams on breathable waders are made waterproof by the application of seam tape on the interior of the wader. A leak means that the bond between the tape and the wader fabric has failed somewhere. One repair expert suggested the following sequence of repair methods, beginning with the simplest and moving down the list as needed.

Seam tape has a heat-bonding adhesive backing, much like iron-on repair material, and the first and easiest repair approach is to reactivate this bond. Turn on an iron to a low-steam, polyester/rayon setting. Turn the waders inside out, and lay the leaking seam flat on an ironing board. Place the iron on the seam, applying gentle pressure for about 10 seconds. Remove the heat and rub up and down the seam tape with another piece of fabric or something smooth such as the side of a plastic ballpoint pen to keep pressure on the tape as it cools. Small seam leaks can often be repaired this way.

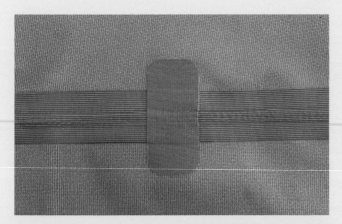

If re-ironing the seam fails, you can apply iron-on patch material if it is supplied or recommended by the manufacturer. Cut a piece of iron-on material about 1½ inches long, and center it crosswise over the leak, as shown here. Affix the patch as explained above in "Iron-on Patches." Press the edge of the iron against the two joints where the patching tape crosses the edges of the original seam tape to get a tight bond.

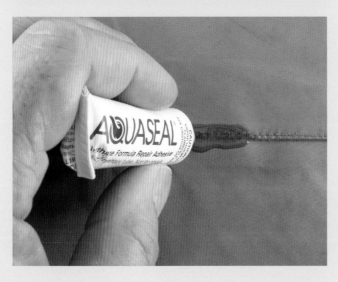

If an iron-on patch fails, Aquaseal usually takes care of the problem. Turn the waders right-side out. Place the opening of the Aquaseal tube flat against the seam joint; squeeze the tube and draw it along the seam over the leaking area, leaving a flat band of adhesive over the joint. If you wish to use an accelerator, you'll have to spread the glue with your fingertip or a small brush, forcing the Aquaseal into the joint between the two pieces of fabric; then put a second, smooth coat of adhesive over the first.

If this fails, you have little recourse but to turn the waders inside out again, and cover the seam tape at the leak with a generous film of Aquaseal, extending the glue outward ½ inch beyond both edges of the seam tape.

NEOPRENE WADERS AND BOOTIES. Here the seam is made waterproof primarily by gluing the material together; that is, unlike the sewn seams on breathable fabrics, the joint between the two pieces of neoprene is itself watertight, though tape is generally applied over the seam as well. A leak means that the two pieces of neoprene beneath the tape have separated or developed a small channel between them that allows water to come through. You may be able to repair a small leak or seep as explained above, by applying a film of Aquaseal over the seam tape on the inside of the wader, outside, or both.

A larger leak, however, means a bigger separation in the neoprene, and you may need to address this kind of damage by regluing the seam itself. And in fact, the technique explained here can be used on any type of wader where you see the seam tape peeling or separating from the wader fabric.

STEP 1: Working from one edge, peel the seam tape away from the wader fabric at the point or area of the leak. Most neoprene seams are taped on both sides, and you can peel the tape from either side; it's worth taking a moment to see if the tape appears looser on one side or the other, and then working from that side. If you have trouble getting the tape to start separating from the wader, try using a warm (not hot) iron to soften the glue on the back side of the tape.

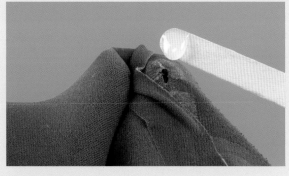

Peel up enough of the tape to get access to the seam. Put your hand inside the wader, and press on the seam from underneath. See if you can detect where the separation has occurred. It may not be a gaping hole; it may just appear as a split partway through the seam, as shown here. If you can see any separation at all, keep some pressure on the seam to keep the gap open, and work some Aquaseal down into the seam.

STEP 2: Then relax pressure with your finger, and spread some Aquaseal over the top of the seam.

You may be able to press the seam tape smoothly back over the seam, but if it

wrinkles or ripples or won't lie flat, you may have stretched or deformed the tape in peeling it back. In this case, lift the tape again. Snip it crosswise in the middle, as shown.

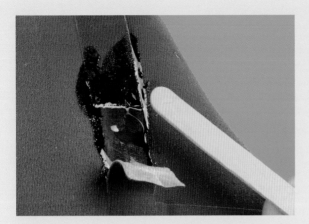

STEP 3: Glue the two flaps down separately, making sure to work some Aquaseal into the joints where the flaps of tape meet the wader fabric. Lay one flap down, and apply adhesive over the surface of the tape, as shown at the top.

STEP 4: Then press down the other flap, and cover the seam tape with a film of Aquaseal, as shown. Use a moistened finger to smooth out the glue, and keep the repair level until it dries.

BOOTFOOT LEAKS

Leaks in the boot of bootfoot waders, particularly small punctures or rips, can be mended with a dab of Aquaseal placed over the damage. Larger repairs may profit from a patch. One repair person told me that he has had success simply by placing a piece of duct tape over the damage and cementing the edges of the tape with Aquaseal; this type of repair, he said, has lasted for years. You can also use a tougher patch, such as a section cut from an inner tube or the material sold to patch whitewater rafts. The important part is that both surfaces—boot and patch—be clean and wiped down with alcohol or Cotol.

Cut a patch to fit. Apply Aquaseal over the damage, and wait about five minutes until the glue is tacky. Press the patch firmly into the glue, and then run a bead of Aquaseal around the edge of the patch to seal it down.

FIELD FIXES

Most wader repairs are simple enough that the techniques explained above can be used even in the field—provided you bring along repair materials. In the absence of the proper equipment, however, or for quick fixes on the water, here are a few tips.

PINHOLE LEAKS

To locate a pinhole leak when you're on the water, you may able to use the sun as your flashlight. Hold the suspected area of damage up to the sun and look for a bright spot shining through.

You can also locate a leak by holding the waders open at the top and capturing air inside or letting the wind inflate them. Bunch up the wader top to hold in the air. Then squeeze the waders to increase the air pressure inside, and immerse them in still water—a lake or a calm spot in the river (or in a tub of water at home). Watch for a tiny stream of bubbles that marks the leak.

You can quickly, if temporarily, fix a small leak like this with a stick of ferrule cement that is used in rod building; I keep one of these in my own repair kit. Get the waders as dry as you can, exposing them to the sun or hanging them in a breeze. Heat the end of the stick with a match or lighter, and wipe the liquefied adhesive over the pinhole. I always apply the cement on the exterior of the wader so that when I return home, I can put a permanent patch on the inside surface, which hasn't been contaminated with any residue from the adhesive. I've had some patches of this type last for months, others only a day or so, depending on how clean and dry the patching surface was.

RIPS AND TEARS

You may be able to temporarily stop, or at least slow, a larger leak (or a pinhole for that matter) in breathable waders by covering the damage with tape. Again, the surface of the waders should be dry. At a minimum, use duct tape, which is stickier, more flexible, and tougher than most other types. But the best I've found is a tape sold for repairing whitewater rafts; it adheres better than duct tape and is more waterproof. In tape repairs, I usually patch both the inside and outside of the waders to add a little more life to the repair. At best, though, the tape is temporary, and you'll need to effect more permanent repair when you can. Be aware that when you remove the tape, some adhesive residue will remain behind, and it must be removed before a permanent patch is applied. Alcohol will usually remove it, as will Cotol-240.

READY-TO-USE GLUE REPAIR

While this repair can certainly be performed at home, I consider it a "field fix" because, with the proper materials, you can patch your waders streamside and be fishing again in 10 or 15 minutes. This method uses Aquaseal sandwiched between two pieces of special tape—Tenacious Tape, manufactured by the makers of Aquaseal (and also included in the Orvis Wader Repair Kit). Provided the repair is done properly, the adhesive is contained entirely between the two pieces of tape and won't stick to your clothing when you put the waders back on. The Aquaseal will dry and cure while you're fishing. It can be used on both neoprene and breathable waders.

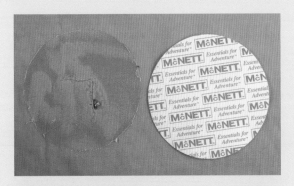

STEP 1: Clean the damaged area and let the wader fabric dry. Cut a piece of Tenacious Tape large enough to overlap the damage by at least ¼ inch on all sides. Peel the paper backing off the tape. Center the tape over the damage, and rub with your fingertip, using a circular motion to press the tape firmly against the outside of the waders, as shown at the left. A matching piece of tape, still attached to the backing, is shown at the right.

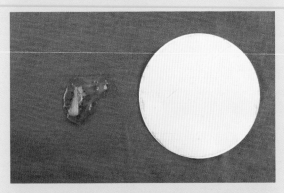

STEP 2: Turn the wader inside out. Smear a film of Aquaseal over the damaged area, as shown. It should extend at least ¼ inch beyond all edges of the damage.

STEP 3: Cut a second piece of Tenacious Tape, large enough to extend ½ inch beyond the edges of the wet Aquaseal. Center the tape over the Aquaseal, and apply it directly atop the wet adhesive. Smooth the tape with your fingertip so that there are no wrinkles or bubbles. If some Aquaseal squeezes out from beneath the tape, wipe it off, or cut an additional small piece of tape to cover the wet adhesive. The object here is to use the tape to form a barrier between the wet Aquaseal and your clothing.

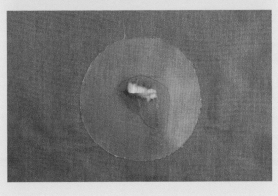

At this point, you're back in business and can continue fishing. After the Aquaseal cures, you can remove the tape or simply leave it in place.

CHAPTER FIVE

WADING BOOTS

P ERHAPS BECAUSE WE ARE ALREADY ACCUSTOMED TO the fact that footwear does not last forever, most anglers don't harbor unrealistic expectations about the life span of wading boots. Our boots see particularly hard service—perhaps harder than any other piece of equipment. They are subject to continual cycles of wetting and drying; abrasion from rocks and dirt; flexes and strains, stresses and torques, and general abuse.

At the same time, wading boots are arguably the single item of gear most directly related to safety on the water, so it's worth taking more than just a passing interest in their upkeep to maximize their useful life and maintain them in good condition.

PREVENTION

● As with waders, the first key in getting the most out of your boots is to buy the proper size. Wearing overly tight boots is not only uncomfortable, but also places undue stress on boot seams—particularly those that attach any sidewall material around the perimeter of the foot and the welt seams that attach the boot upper to the sole. As noted earlier, boots that are too large allow your foot to slip around inside, promoting abrasion on wader booties and decreasing security and sure-footedness in wading. When you go to purchase wading boots, take along your waders and any wading socks you might wear to make sure the boots comfortably accommodate the extra thickness.

Getting a good fit is not always easy, since the sizes and widths of wading boots are usually more limited than those of ordinary street shoes. If your foot falls between sizes, it's better to wear boots that are slightly larger rather than smaller. I've had success fine-tuning the fit by using commercially available cushioned insoles made of waterproof, high-density synthetic material.

They take up any slack on the inside of the boot and improve overall comfort significantly.

- With their thick soles, rigid toes and heels, and ankle-supporting uppers, wading boots superficially resemble hiking boots. But they are built for a different purpose. If you routinely walk long distances into rugged country—hiking in and out of steep canyons, or negotiating tough, rocky trails—consider packing in your wading boots and putting them on at the water. Nothing that I know of will blow out side seams on a wading boot faster than mountain-goating through rough terrain. At the very least, it prematurely wears out felt soles and grinds down studded ones.

- Avoid leaving your wading boots in direct sunlight or a hot car trunk for extended periods of time. Ultraviolet rays and excessive heat gradually degrade virtually any wading boot material.

CARE AND MAINTENANCE

From a maintenance standpoint, wading boots are pretty straightforward. The two biggest enemies are grit and moisture.

Wading boots, practically by definition, are going to get dirty, and there's not much you can do about it. But you can take measures to keep them from staying dirty. Sand and dirt is deposited into seams, stitching, and the weave of fabrics such as nylon that are sometimes used to construct the boot uppers. These particles of grit are sharp, and as the boot is flexed in wading and walking, the abrasive particles grind away at stitches and woven materials, abrading and weakening them.

When you return home from a day's fishing, hose off your boots, removing as much surface dirt as you can from uppers and seam areas; spraying off the laces helps prolong their life as well. Rinse out any pebbles and sand from the inside of the boot to help protect your waders. And it is absolutely crucial to rinse boots as soon as possible after they are used in salt water to prevent corrosion of eyelet, speed-lace, and other metal components. Then dry the boots. I usually tie the laces together and hang them up on a nail so that air circulates freely all around them. Boots that are left wet can mildew.

CHECKUP

Few anglers, in my experience, give much thought to their boots until a problem develops, which is almost always on the water—a seam that pulls out, a small crack that develops into a full-blown split or hole, a sole that comes loose. But spending a moment once or twice a season to check over your boots can alert you to problems that are still in the early stages before a small repair job turns into a big one, or the damage is so far along that no repair is possible at all. And it's especially advisable to check your boots before taking off on an extended trip. While packing along a backup rod, reel, line, and even waders is standard practice, the added weight and bulk often makes bringing an extra pair of boots impractical, particularly with air travel.

Clean and dry your boots, and begin by inspecting the uppers. Many uppers are constructed of woven material, usually a heavy-duty nylon, and reinforced in high-stress or high-wear areas with natural or synthetic leather or a rubberlike material. Check the woven fabric for any rips, holes, or abraded areas. If the materials used to reinforce the uppers are sewn on, check the stitches for broken, frayed, or loose threads. Look closely at the seams securing any material on which eyelets are mounted and at seams where the uppers are sewn to reinforcing material at the toe, heel, and edges of the boot. Pay particular attention to any seams at the outside edge of the boot—the single most common spot for a seam to split. Put one hand inside the boot, right down to the toe, and use the other hand to try to peel the boot sole away from the upper, looking closely at the seam that joins them to make sure that it is intact. If the boot uses glued construction—usually with rubber toe caps and sidewalls—check to make sure that the glued seam is secure. If the boot is made of natural or synthetic leather, check for splits, cracks, or deep abrasions that may be developing, typically at the toe or outside edge of the boot.

Examine the eyelets or speed-lace hardware to make sure they aren't pulling free from the upper or tearing the material on which they are mounted. Look at the laces as well to see if they are thin or fraying. Then check the ankle of the boot to see if the seams around the boot opening and those securing any ankle padding are tight and in good condition.

Inspect the felt soles closely, working your way around the perimeter of the boot to make sure the sole is not coming unglued anywhere. Use your thumb to try to peel the felt from the bottom of the boot, and see if you can detect any gaps between the felt and the boot sole—especially at the toe, where most felts first begin to work free. Once this kind of delamination begins, it gets worse rather quickly.

Finally, examine the condition of the felt to see if the soles need replacement. This is admittedly a bit of a judgment call. Certainly if the felt is worn down at the edge far enough that the sole of the boot is exposed and beginning to wear, the felts should be replaced. If the corners of the boot sole itself become rounded with wear, getting a tight joint between the sole and a fresh pair of felts is more difficult. If the soles are visibly thin, they should be replaced.

Most anglers don't consider replacing their felts until they are worn extremely thin or begin to come off the boot. Fair enough, I suppose, but wading boots are a little like fly lines; performance declines so gradually that we often don't even notice it. After a time, the compression force from standing and walking in your boots compacts the felt and grinds particles of sand and dirt into the soles. The felt becomes hard and smooth on the bottom, giving less bite on streambed rocks, even though the soles have not yet worn noticeably thin and are still firmly attached to the boots. How much loss of traction you are willing to tolerate is, of course, an individual matter and must be weighed against the work involved in replacing the soles. But there's no question that fresh felts improve wading security and make standing and walking more comfortable.

REPAIR

First, the bad news. Many types of wading boot damage are not really feasible for home repair; the tools required are too specialized, and you'll get the best results anyway by taking your boots to a shoe-repair person or returning them to a manufacturer who offers repair services. In most cases, a shoe-repair shop can restitch seams where the uppers join reinforcing material under the eyelets; around the sidewalls of the boot; and at the toe, heel, or ankle—provided the damage is not so extensive that the integrity of the fabric has degraded to the point where it won't hold a stitch. Usually, a shop can also patch splits or holes in the uppers of boots made of woven material or synthetic or natural leather and can replace lost or broken lacing eyelets and hardware. And I've had a shop reglue separating seams between uppers and rubber toes and sidewalls. Unfortunately, if a side seam between the uppers and the topsole splits out—typically on the outside edge of the foot—not much can be done; there isn't enough intact fabric left on the uppers to resew them, and most repair shops aren't equipped for that kind of procedure anyway.

In my experience, shoe-repair shops vary rather widely in their willingness to work on wading boots. The repairs sometimes fall outside their usual realm of experience and must be improvised, and some shops are reluctant to attempt a repair that they cannot say with some certainty will be effective. Still, it's always worth checking with a repair shop or the manufacturer to see if the boots can be mended.

If a local repair person declines to do the job, you may have one last resort. I've found that shoe-repair shops in high-traffic angling destinations are often more experienced with, and willing to work on, wading boots. They simply get asked a lot and have developed methods. If I'm traveling to fish southwest Montana, for instance, I'll bring a pair of damaged boots along and shop them around to see if I can find someone who's willing to do the job (always, of course, bringing a second pair of usable boots in case I can't find any takers or the work requires a few days).

Repairing felt soles or replacing them altogether is a different matter, however, and one that is entirely feasible to accomplish at home. But in the interests of honest and full disclosure, I must admit that when my felts need replacing, I take them first to a shoe shop; a professional can usually do the job faster, in most cases better, and in all cases with less effort that you can do it at home. The charge is generally reasonable, though if you take this route, you will have to supply new felt soles of the proper size yourself since repair shops don't stock them. Or again, you can check with the manufacturer to see if resoling is available.

But many repair shops will not resole wading boots, and none that I know of will put new felts on bootfoot waders (I'm not sure why), and so the job falls to you.

REMOVING WORN SOLES

Resoling your wading boots or bootfoots actually has two parts, and the first (removing the old soles) is sometimes a bigger challenge than the second (attaching new ones). Taking off the old soles may require some improvisation, but you can eventually get the job done.

Before removing the soles, however, take a look at the beginning of the next section, "Resoling Boots," to find which style of wading boot or bootfoot you have so that you can attach the new soles in the proper way. Once the old soles are removed, you won't have them as a reminder.

Though I've talked to repair experts, and experimented a good deal myself over the last three decades, I must confess that I've never discovered a quick and simple way to remove old felt soles. The two basic approaches explained below are the most commonly used, and with patience both will work equally well with wading boots and bootfoot waders.

Regardless of the method, however, first make sure the boots are clean and completely dry. Clean uppers are important; after gluing the new sole is clamped with tape until it dries, and the tape may not adhere well to dirty uppers. Stuff boots tightly with wadded-up newspaper, packing it firmly into the toes and up the ankles. The newspaper adds stiffness and makes the boot easier to handle when removing the old felt and tape-clamping the new sole in place. If the boots have laces, tie them tightly to compact the newspaper and keep them out of the way.

GRINDING. The first method, grinding the sole, requires a bench grinder; a grinding wheel mounted in an electric drill will also work, though it will slow down a process that is already fairly slow. The object here is simply to use the wheel to shred off the old felt. This takes times—the felt is surprisingly resistant—but you can speed it up a little by using a very coarse grinding wheel with a wide face. It does get rather messy, since the wheel spins off felt fibers, and it is (with the exception explained below) most practical with plain, not studded, felt soles. But while grinding may be slow, it is also certain and does a clean job.

As you grind the felt, work back and forth evenly across the sole and heel. When most of the felt is removed, and the boot sole is nearly exposed, work a bit more carefully to grind away the remaining shreds of felt along with any residue of old adhesive. Then use the wheel to abrade the sole of the boot lightly so that it will bond well with the glue. Roughen the sole right out to the edges, but take care not to round off the corners of the boot sole itself; a flat boot sole with nice square corners at the edge gives the best adhesion to the felt.

After the boot sole is abraded, brush away any loose particles; wipe down the sole with alcohol to remove any remaining debris and clean the surface.

Note: Strictly speaking, it isn't necessary to completely remove the old sole. If you grind it away evenly, far enough down that the surface of the felt is clean, you can glue new felts over the tops of the old ones. In fact, stacked-heel boots (pictured on page 142) use this felt-on-felt approach in construction. But the key here—and the caution—is that the existing felt surface must be very clean to get good adhesion with the glue. Clean felt, of course, isn't a problem when stacked heels are glued up during manufacturing; all the felt is brand new. Gluing over old felt can be a different matter, though; I've had it work, but I've probably had it fail more times. The soles will certainly stay on for a while, but my own feeling is that they are apt to peel off prematurely, and I generally prefer removing the old felt completely. Still, gluing over old felt has worked for me at times, and if you are reasonably sure that you've ground off enough felt to give a smooth, clean surface, this method may save you some time. This approach will also work with many types of studded felts; just grind down the studs along with the felt so that everything is flush, and you can glue the new soles right over the top of the old ones, studs and all.

STRIPPING. The second approach, stripping the sole, is somewhat faster and doesn't require a bench grinder (though it is still handy to have one for the latter stages of this method). Stripping is also the best way to completely remove old studded felt soles, since grinding away old cleats can be extremely tedious. In this technique, you simply use a strong pair of pliers and sharp utility knife to peel the felt from the boot sole—it's a little like skinning a deer. The key here is getting an initial grip on the felt.

If the felt has already begun to peel away from the sole anywhere around the perimeter, you're in business; this will be the access point at which you begin stripping the sole.

But if the felt is still firmly bonded to the boot, you'll have to fashion your own starting point by detaching a flap of felt from the boot sole. You can create this flap by using a utility knife to carefully slice along the glue seam between the boot sole and the felt. Beginning at the toe of the boot is usually easiest. Use only moderate pressure on the knife blade, and make repeated strokes along the same line, gradually enlarging the depth of the cut. It isn't necessary to slice exactly along the glue seam; you can leave a thin film of felt attached to the boot sole and remove it later. You don't need to raise a large of flap of felt—just enough to grab with the pliers.

Once you've got an access point, use the pliers to roll the flap of felt rearward. Keep it under tension as you slice along the joint between the boot sole and the felt. Holding the boot steady, maintaining pressure on the pliers, and cutting with a knife may prove to be more than two hands can easily manage. Enlisting the assistance of another person simplifies the job, but you can also clamp the boot upside down in a bench vise to hold it still.

Stripping a sole like this does not go rapidly, but it does go steadily. Once the sole is peeled off, you should remove any remaining felt and old adhesive from the boot sole. A grinding wheel makes short work of it, but you can also use a coarse wood rasp or an electric sander with coarse paper. As noted above, take care to keep the edges of the boot sole as square as possible to give the best bond with the new felt. When the sole is clean, wipe it down with alcohol, and you're ready to mount the new felts.

RESOLING BOOTS

Most wading boots and bootfoot waders can be resoled. But boot designs differ, and it's worth taking note of the type you have in order to purchase the proper materials and maintain the original sole style. Boots typically use one of the four following sole designs:

Boots with one-piece soles use a single, continuous piece of felt to cover the entire boot bottom. Some older-style boots simply have a flat sole from toe to heel, and these are the simplest to resole. Modern boots, however, are more likely to incorporate a sole that is molded with a distinct heel, as shown here. This design, with a flat front sole and a beveled portion up to the heel, can be a bit tricky to resole. Getting the new felt to conform tightly to the boot sole as it bends up the bevel and over the heel depends on the particular shape of the sole and the flexibility of the felt replacement. But this is a widely used design, and so a boot of this type is used in the following demonstration. Fortunately, the task can be addressed in a couple of ways—resoling with a single piece of felt, as shown in the main photo sequence, or resoling with two pieces as shown in the photo on page 148. You may wish to consult that photo before resoling the boots to see if the alternate approach shown there appears simpler to you.

Some boots use a stacked heel, built up from one or more additional pieces of felt. These are relatively simple to resole using the procedure shown in the following demonstration, but they do require a special sole-replacement kit that contains extra heel pieces.

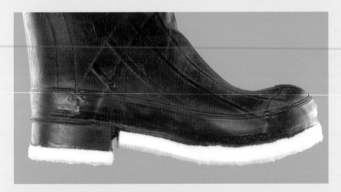

Raised-heel boots, often found on bootfoot waders such as the ones shown here, have a separate, distinctly elevated heel. In resoling, the front and heel portions are attached independently according to the instructions below. The heel piece is formed by cutting off the rear section of a one-piece felt replacement sole.

Inset soles are recessed between rubber bumpers at the front and rear, as shown here. The bumpers shield the front and back edges of the felt to help prevent it from peeling off the boot. The felt inserts are simply cut from a one-piece replacement sole. The key in resoling this design is trimming the new felts to fit between the bumpers, as shown below in Step 2a.

To resole wading boots or bootfoots, you'll need:

- Replacement soles. These are available at fly shops and sporting good stores, and are sold in sizes. You want a new sole that is about ¼ inch or more larger, all the way around the edge, than the existing sole. If in doubt, buy a larger size; you can cut it down when the time comes. Remember that if you're replacing a stacked-heel boot, you'll need a replacement with extra heel sections.

- Cement for gluing. Contact cement is commonly used for resoling, and some soles are sold in kits with this type of adhesive included. But you want to be generous with the glue, and I've found that even the large 4-ounce tube sometimes contained in these kits is not quite enough for the job. I recommend buying additional cement; Barge brand is one that is commonly used.

    Recently, two-part adhesives have become available for resoling wading boots. These make the glue job go a little faster, though actual drying time is longer than that required by contact cement. The downside to these two-part glues is a surprisingly fast set-time; you need to have everything in readiness before the glue is mixed, and then work efficiently. A delay of any length of time may allow the adhesive to thicken to the point that it is unusable.

    For your first attempt at resoling, I suggest contact cement; the greater working time will not force you to rush the job.

- A Popsicle-type stick or disposable brush for spreading the cement. A brush ½ to ¼ inch wide is fine, but it should have stiff bristles; the cement is thick. If the bristles are soft, trim off the ends to shorten and stiffen them.

- Felt-tipped pen.

- Duct tape.

- Utility knife with a sharp blade.

- You may also want a piece of wood, cut to size as shown in Step 8, to aid in clamping the new felt.

STEP 1: Remove the old felts and clean the soles as explained in "Removing Worn Soles," page 139. Leave the boots stuffed with newspaper. This boot had a one-piece, studded sole. The round marks on the sole were left by the base of the cleats. The new felt will simply be applied right over them.

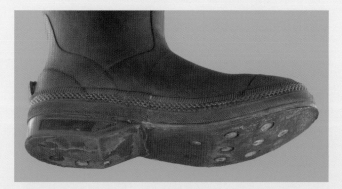

STEP 2: Test-fit the felt sole to the boot by centering the boot on the new sole. If your boot uses a one-piece sole design of the type shown here, with a bevel at the arch, place a spacer—a length of wooden dowel, a ballpoint, or, as shown here, the handle of an X-Acto knife—to force the felt up into the wedge and conform to the sole. In the next step, you'll trace an outline of the boot on the new felt, and you want to include the extra sole length needed to cover this beveled area. If the boot sole is flat, there is no need for this spacer. If your boot has an inset sole, see Step 3a.

It's possible that the new felt will not conform closely to this angled portion of the sole. The sole may be too stiff and refuse to bend, or the bevel may be too steep, or both. In this case, you may be better off adopting the approach shown at the end of this sequence, where the forward portion of the sole and the heel are covered with separate pieces of felt, just as in a raised-heel design. If the new felt does not fit tightly against the angle in the sole, the glue joint may prove weak, and the sole may prematurely separate at this point.

STEP 3: Ideally, when you place the boot on the new sole, the felt should extend about ¼ inch beyond all edges of the boot sole. A piece of felt that overhangs the edges of the sole too far can interfere with tape-clamping the felt after gluing. If the new sole is too big—all the way around or just at certain points—use a marking pen to draw a line ¼ inch beyond the edge of the boot; this line will be a guide in trimming away the excess felt material.

Some boots, especially on bootfoot waders, are made with a slightly upturned toe, and some older boots will acquire this curvature with use. When tracing around the toe of such a boot, it's important to rock the boot forward so that the toe portion lies flat against the new felt sole. Tracing around an upturned toe may result in the replacement sole being too short.

Here, a line has been traced around the parts of the sole that are overly large. The felt fits well through the middle of the boot but is too long at the heel and toe. The black line shows where the excess material will be cut away.

If the boot requires a separate piece of felt for the heel, or uses a stacked heel design, repeat the process, tracing any outline needed around the heel portions.

Then use a sharp utility knife to cut away the excess felt, as shown. Once one of the soles (and heels if any) is trimmed to the proper shape, you can use it as a template to trace a line on the second sole, and then trim away the excess felt.

STEP 3a: If your boots have inset soles, you'll need to trim a piece of felt—at both the forward portion of the sole and the heel—to fit between the rubber bumpers. If you used the stripping method to remove the old sole, and the sole is still intact, you can use it as a template to trace an outline on the replacement felt sole. If you ground off the old sole, you'll have to make a paper template.

Note that the front and rear edges of the new felt, as shown here, should be trimmed to fit just inside the bumpers. The outer edges of the sole that are not confined by bumpers, however, are left with a ¼ inch overhang on each side of the boot.

STEP 4: The new soles here will be affixed using contact cement. Ordinarily contact cement is applied to both surfaces and allowed to dry for a short time before joining them together. But because felt is absorbent, there's an intermediate step that needs to be taken.

Apply some glue to one of the felt soles, using a brush or wooden stick to spread it all across the sur-

face of the sole. Make certain to get glue out to the very edges of the felt. You don't want an excessively thick layer, but don't be stingy with the adhesive. Give it a good, uniform coating. Then coat the other felt sole and any separate heels.

Let the glue dry for at least half an hour and up to several hours. The idea here is to let the felt absorb what glue it will, and then dry. This glue provides a nonabsorbent base layer for a second application of adhesive that actually attaches the replacement sole to the boot.

If you're using a two-part adhesive, this step isn't necessary.

At this point, tear 8 to 10 foot-long strips of duct tape; attach them by one end to the edge of your worktable or bench, letting them hang downward. When it comes time to clamp the new sole, it's helpful to have the tape strips ready at hand.

STEP 5: After the glue on the felt dries, apply a second layer of glue, spreading it to the very edges of one of the new soles. Then apply a layer of glue to the corresponding boot sole, again making sure the adhesive extends to the very edge of the boot sole. You want a

good glue bond at the edges of the boot since this is the point at which soles typically work loose and begin to separate.

Let this application of adhesive on both felt and boot sole dry for about 10 minutes, or the length of time specified by the glue manufacturer.

Once the glue is tacky, carefully press the heel portion of the felt to the heel of the boot, as shown. Don't allow the front of the felt sole to touch the boot.

Two-part adhesives are typically applied to the boot sole only, and the felt is laid in place immediately after.

STEP 6: Now press the felt sole firmly against the bevel on the boot sole. Press it very tightly so that the felt "turns the corners" sharply at the top and bottom of the beveled area. You want the felt to conform as closely as possible to the contour of the boot bottom.

On boots with flat bottoms, insets, or raised heels, this step won't be necessary since there is no bevel on the sole. Just join the entire felt sole to the boot sole.

STEP 7: Finally press the felt against the forward portion of the boot sole.

Duct tape is used to hold the replacement felt in place and provide clamping pressure for a good bond. Apply the tape as follows:

Center a strip crosswise over the sole. On the type of sole shown here, place this first piece of tape at the base of the bevel on the sole, as shown. (On soles without a bevel, begin at the middle of the sole.) Press the tape against the middle of the felt, then pull one end of the tape outward, then very firmly downward, as shown, forcing the edge of the felt tightly against the edge of the boot sole. Then stick the tape to the boot upper to hold it in place. Repeat with the other end of the tape strip. By applying downward pressure at the edge of the felt sole, this method promotes a tighter, closer bond at the edge of the boot sole—where a weak joint can lead to delamination—than you can get by simply spiraling a strip of tape around and around the boot.

STEP 8: Perhaps you have sensed by now that I am a little paranoid about getting a tight glue joint at the beveled portion of the sole. To get the best bond possible, I cut a piece of wood to help maximize a uniform clamping pressure over this area. The piece of wood is long enough to run the length of the bevel and just wide enough to cover the beveled area from side to side, as shown.

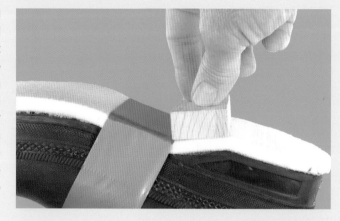

STEP 9: Position this piece of wood evenly over the bevel, and then secure it in a very tight wrap of duct tape using the procedure explained in the previous step.

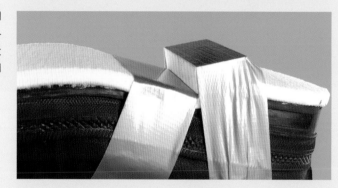

STEP 10: Continue wrapping strips of tape over the entire surface of the felt and around the boot using the method shown in Step 6.

After the entire sole is taped, check the first tape strips you applied and see if they are still tight. As you apply the tape, you will gradually compress the boot upper, and this compression may cause some of the first strips to develop slack. If that is the case, apply new strips of tape over the old ones to reestablish clamping pressure on the sole.

When the first boot is finished, glue and tape the second. At this point, your boots will be almost completely covered in tape, as shown. Let the glue dry for at least 12 hours, and longer certainly doesn't hurt. (Two-part glues may take longer.)

STEP 11: When the drying time is up, remove the tape from the boot, and trim away the excess felt extending beyond the edge of the boot sole. You can remove this excess with a grinder pretty easily, but cutting it away with a utility knife, using the edge of the boot sole as a guide, works fine.

If, in Step 1 of this procedure, you were unable to get the felt sole to conform to the angle in the boot, you can certainly take this alternate approach.

Though your boot was manufactured with a single piece of felt on the sole, you can easily resole it with two pieces of felt, one on the forward part of the sole, one on the heel, just as in the raised-heel design shown on page 142. You do lose a little surface area of felt on the bottom of the sole, but the boots will work just fine. On this boot, the bevel is steep and short. I was concerned that a one-piece replacement sole might not bond seamlessly against the beveled area, so I used the two-piece approach.

LOOSE SOLES

A felt sole rarely just falls off all of a sudden. It works loose by degrees, usually separating first at the toe, producing a loose flap of felt that gets larger and larger as you walk and wade. It's not only annoying, but dangerous; when the flap gets big enough, it catches on rocks and brush and can easily cause you to trip. If the sole is otherwise in good condition, you may wish to repair rather than replace it.

It's possible to reglue a partially separated sole by using the same technique explained above for resoling a boot. The tricky part is in getting the gluing surfaces clean. And they'll probably be pretty dirty; a loose flap tends to capture dirt and debris as you walk and wade, wedging it into the joint between the felt and the boot sole. If the separation is small, a flap of felt only an inch or two long, it's difficult to get enough working room to clean the surfaces, though it can be done. A larger separation gives better access. The cleaning is the same in either case.

Begin by thoroughly washing the boot sole and the back side of the felt with soapy water. Use a small brush such as a toothbrush, to scrub the gluing surfaces, working particularly to clean out the joint area where the felt is still affixed to the boot. Then let the boot dry completely; since felt readily absorbs water, drying can take up to a few days.

When the boot is dry, rough up the boot sole with sandpaper or a wood rasp. Glue and tape the sole as described earlier. In this case, however, it won't be necessary to apply an initial layer of cement to the felt as described above in Step 4; this layer of glue was applied when the original sole was attached to the boot, and you can begin with Step 5.

The truth of the matter is that, while this method can yield a lasting repair, it's not uncommon for the sole to separate again in the same place since dirt that becomes embedded in the back side of the felt may prohibit a strong glue bond. To make the repair more durable, I prefer to go one step beyond gluing and actually screw the felt to the boot sole. This type of repair can be performed anywhere that the felt has begun to separate from the boot sole, but it's particularly useful at the toe. It adds extra holding power where the felt sole is most prone to separate. In fact, I have omitted the glue on a number of occasions, and the screws hold fine.

This approach does, however, have its limits. First, it relies on getting screws of the proper size. They must be long enough to go completely through the felt and into the boot sole, but not so long that they penetrate the insole of the boot, where they will shred your wader booties in short order. And second, I don't recommend it for bootfoot waders. The wading boots used with stockingfoot waders tend to have thicker soles, sometimes with a "lip" as shown in Step 2 below; it's easier to estimate the screw length on such boots, and should you accidentally drill or screw through to the inside of the boot, no harm is done. The waders themselves will still keep you dry. If, on the other hand, you drill through or puncture the boots on bootfoot waders, water will enter.

STEP 1: The length of the screw depends upon the thickness of the existing felt and the thickness of the boot sole. Once the sole is glued back in place, measure to find the screw length that will go through the felt and reach about a third of the way into the boot sole, as shown here. This sole has separated at the toe, and so the screw length is gauged at this part of the sole. As you might expect, it's better to err here on the short side; you can get a little extra bite from a short screw as explained below by driving it in hard enough to compress the felt.

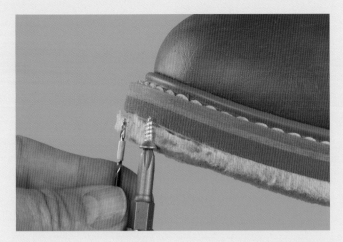

I've found that #6 wood or sheet metal screws, ranging in length from about ⅜ to ½ inch, will cover most situations. Thicker screws are harder to drive in and have coarse threads with less bite; thinner screws have overly fine and shallow threads that can pull out. I like flathead or panhead screws that seat flush with the surface of the felt, though almost any type can be used. Stainless-steel screws are a good idea, especially for boots used in salt water.

To install the screws, you'll need to drill pilot holes slightly smaller than the diameter of the screw, or punch them with an awl. To avoid drilling all the way through the boot sole to the inside of the boot, wrap a piece of masking tape around the drill bit to mark the proper pilot-hole depth, as shown.

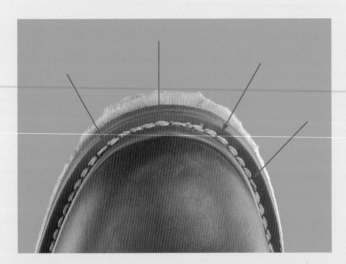

STEP 2: Wading boots are constructed in various ways, but if your boots have a sole that extends outward beyond the upper, you can drive the screws into this "lip" to keep the screw point safely away from the inner sole and your wader booties. The screw, obviously, comes from underneath, but the arrow here shows the part of the sole into which it is fastened. If your boots don't have this lip, you can still install screws; just choose the screw length carefully.

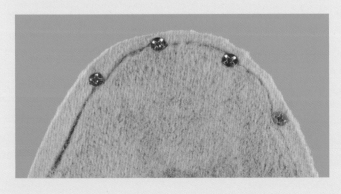

STEP 3: The number and spacing of screws is for the most part a matter of choice. When the felt is separated just at the toe, I use three or four closely spaced screws. The screws farthest from the toe on either side of the sole are located at the joint where the felt is still affixed to the boot sole. The remaining

screws are placed at about 1-inch intervals. Keep the screws as close to the edge of the felt sole as possible.

If the screws are a little on the short side, drive them very firmly into the sole, compressing the felt to get extra bite into the boot sole.

When you're finished, make sure to put your hand inside the boot and feel the foot bed. If the screw point has raised a small bump on the insole, but hasn't broken through, remove it and try a shorter screw. Pressure from walking can eventually work the point of the screw through the insole into your wader booties.

I've found this to be quite a durable repair. Even stainless screws, however, will eventually corrode, though they may well last for the life of the sole or of the boot.

CRACKS, SPLITS, ABRASION, AND FRAY

As noted earlier damage to the boot uppers and seams—both synthetic leather and woven materials—are best addressed by a shoe-repair person, who can actually mend them. But you can at least forestall further damage yourself by applying an adhesive such as Aquaseal or Goop to cracks or splits in synthetic leather, abraded areas on woven uppers, and anywhere that stitching is beginning to fray or come loose or has broken. The main concern in getting a strong repair is that the surface of the boot be as clean and dry as possible for good adhesion. The adhesive is applied just as you would use it to patch waders, but spread it on liberally. Such patches can hold for a surprisingly long time, though in the end they may need renewing.

FIELD FIXES

If home repairs to wading boots are somewhat limited, field fixes are even more so, and they tend to be rather primitive and temporary.

SEAMS

The worst kind of wading shoe breakdown that I know of is a blown seam on the side of the boot. It typically begins in the vicinity of the little toe; without support, your foot slides inside the boot, and the rip gets bigger and bigger. About the only remedy that will keep you fishing is taping the boot to keep the upper attached to the sole.

You can use duct tape or fiberglass packing tape for this, but as noted in the chapter on waders, the kind of tape used for whitewater raft repair is stickier, tougher, and more waterproof. The tape will adhere better if the boot is dry, but I've taped up wet boots on more than one occasion. Simply take wraps of tape around the boot, crossing the area of the torn seam. Pull the tape tight to help prevent your foot from shifting around inside. Try to use the thinnest strip of tape that will do the job, tearing the tape lengthwise if necessary, to minimize the amount of felt sole covered over with tape. The taped areas, of course, provide no traction on the streambed. And if you use too much tape, you may have to remove it to expose enough of the laces to get your boot off. But realistically speaking, broad strips of tape may be the only way to hold your boots together, and retaping them for each use may be the only option.

LOOSE SOLES

Glue repairs to wading boot soles aren't terribly practical in the field, unless you have a day or two to spend letting your felts dry out. But you can reattach a felt sole that is partially separated from the boot if you pack your repair kit wisely; carrying a selection of screws in assorted lengths will allow you to screw the sole to the boot as described earlier. In this case, of course, you won't be gluing the sole first—just fastening it with the screws. And in fact, I have reattached soles that have come completely off the boot this way. Since it's unlikely you'll have access to an electric drill, pack an ordinary finishing nail in your repair kit; you can use it to pound a pilot hole through the felt and into the boot sole.

A separated sole can also be temporarily held with tape. If the separation is at the toe of the boot, run a strip or two of tape from the sole, over the toe, and onto the upper. Then wrap tape crosswise around the boot to secure the ends of the strips protecting the toe.

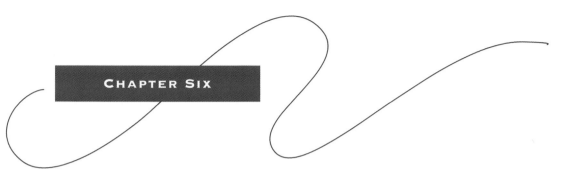

CHAPTER SIX

OTHER STUFF

RODS AND REELS, LINES, WADERS AND BOOTS—these typically represent the core of a fly-fishing outfit and, where care and maintenance are concerned, the gear to which we usually turn our attention. But other, less obvious items of our equipment profit as well from upkeep that extends their life or improves performance.

FLIES

Anglers are apt to regard individual flies as pretty much disposable commodities, and there's no question that fish, snags, trees, and general wear and tear take their toll on our fly boxes during the season. Still, were you to sit down and total it up, you might well discover that of all the stuff you carry in your vest, flies represent the single largest investment. And there is no reason that they should suffer from unnecessary neglect or damage that shortens their life or compromises their fishing effectiveness.

PREVENTION

I ask your indulgence in the first few points here, as I am something of a fanatic on the matter. But as a fly tyer, I am often appalled at how anglers sometimes store and carry their flies—particularly dry flies.

- The single best way to store dry flies is in a compartmented fly box. Carrying collar-hackle patterns (such as the Adams or Quill Gordon) or palmer-hackle ones (such as the Elk Hair Caddis or Stimulator) in a foam fly box or other type of box that holds the flies flush against the box interior almost invariably crushes or folds the hackle. This is more than a matter of mere aesthetics, since flies that are distorted like this may not sit properly on the water; they may float on their sides, facedown, or in other positions that present an un-natural silhouette to the trout. But even other types of dry flies (parachute patterns, no-hackle styles, and so on) are apt to end up with bent wings or tails when stored in such boxes, deforming the basic architecture of the pattern and rendering it potentially less attractive to the fish. Save foam and flat-storage boxes for nymphs, wets, and streamers.

- For the same reason, don't overcrowd fly-box compartments; closing the lid can mash the more delicate components.

- Pinning dry flies on a fleece fly patch or hatband is another sure way to bend them out of shape. Instead, carry a small, empty plastic box (it doesn't need to be compartmented) in your vest; when you change flies, put the used patterns in this box. When the day is finished, simply open the lid and let the flies dry out before returning them to your regular fly boxes. Dry flies won't be crushed, and the box is far more secure, especially for larger flies and weighted nymphs, which tend to work loose and fall off fleece patches.

- Probably the biggest threats to flies are rust and corrosion. Individual flies can rust if they are put away wet—particularly if they are stored in foam boxes. Moisture trapped between the hook wire and the foam evaporates very slowly, and the hook bend can begin to rust.

- A potentially more serious problem is a fly box that has become wet on the inside—dropped in the water, exposed to rain, or left open to spray or splash in a boat. I know from firsthand experience that you can lose an entire box of flies to corrosion if they are put away wet and forgotten. If you get water in a fly box, dump out any standing water right away, and go back to your fishing; rust isn't going to set in instantly. But when the day is over, dry out the fly box and the flies. If the box is compartmented, open it up and put it in a sunny window, in front of a heating or air-conditioning vent, or anywhere there is circulating air, though everything will dry faster if you empty the flies out of the box.

  If the flies are in a foam fly box or any type of box that uses clips, slots, pegs, bristles, nubs, or fleece to the hold the hooks, you are infinitely better off taking the time to remove all the flies and let them dry. Water is held where contact surfaces, such as clips or foam, touch the hook wires, and rust will form. You might get away with simply opening the lid and hoping for the best, but the only guarantee of avoiding corrosion is taking the flies out of the box.

- Like all equipment used in salt water, flies require extra care. They often represent a larger investment than trout flies—if you tie them yourself, they take more time; if you buy them, they are more expensive. I keep any flies I've used during the day in a separate plastic box and, when I return from fishing, give them a quick rinse when I wash my reel. Certainly, at the end of an extended trip, flies that have been fished should be rinsed and dried, especially patterns that have metal components such as the bead-chain eyes on Crazy Charleys. Left untended, these will corrode in fairly short order.

● Rinsing and drying a box full of saltwater patterns that's been dropped in the water or drenched by spray is a pain, and I prefer to carry saltwater flies in a gasketed, waterproof fly box to avoid the hassle.

I keep larger flies that don't fit well into most fly boxes—big striper patterns, Deceivers, Whistlers, and the like—in individual zip-closing bags, and put those loose bags into a larger zip-closing one. It's not a perfect storage system, but the bags keep the flies flat to minimize crumpling or distorting the wings and tails, and they stay dry.

CARE AND MAINTENANCE

Other than taking precautions to avoid crushing your flies and to prevent rust or corrosion, you don't really need to lavish much attention on them. But there is one potential problem that may occur with long-term storage. Though it is not common, insects such as hide beetles, carpet beetles, and moths can pose a threat to the materials from which the fly is constructed, as anyone who ties flies is well aware. I've seen a few boxes of flies (and once, a framed display of what used to be Atlantic salmon patterns) pretty much reduced to bare hooks and a few scraps of feather by insects. This kind of thing doesn't happen overnight, and I've never seen or heard of it occurring with flies kept in boxes that used are reasonably often. But many anglers have selections of flies that used are only infrequently. My pike and striper patterns, for instance, may sit around for a year or two between fishing trips; protecting them is simple and prudent.

You can keep your flies safe from insect infestation in the off season or during prolonged storage by putting your fly boxes in an airtight plastic food-storage container. You can add a few mothballs, some moth crystals bagged in a piece of nylon stocking material, or—as some fly tyers do—sections cut from a plastic flea collar sold for pets.

If you have the space, you can also protect your flies simply by storing them in a freezer. Freezing not only prevents insect damage, but (at least as a general rule) kills any vermin that might be present.

At the very least, store your flies out of direct sunlight, which can fade colors and accelerate the deterioration of the tying materials.

REPAIR

Any fly that is fished much eventually gets tattered, ragged, and generally beaten up. Even a well-tied fly will not last forever. When the tails or wings or legs on a pattern are broken or bitten off, there isn't much you can do. But a couple of common types of damage can be remedied.

LOOSE THREAD. From time to time, the thread at the head of the fly will become loose and begin to unravel. Because most flies are tied without any knots during construction, the fly will eventually untie itself and come apart. But if you can catch the problem soon enough, you can usually rescue the fly.

If the tag of thread is long enough, you can secure it again with one or more half hitches directly behind the hook eye. Form a loop in the thread tag, slip it over the hook eye, and pull the tag to tighten the knot. If the remaining tag is still long enough, add two or three more half hitches and clip the excess thread. Then use a needle or toothpick to apply a very small drop of head cement, fingernail polish, or liquid cyanoacrylate (CA) glue such as superglue to the thread wraps, taking care not to let the cement bleed into the dressing materials.

If the tag is too short to half-hitch, put some tension on the thread tag. You can, for instance, clip the thread in a pair of hemostats and let them hang beneath the fly. Apply a small drop of liquid CA glue to the thread wraps. If the thread is dry, the glue will penetrate almost instantly and dry quickly. Then clip the excess thread tag.

CRUSHED OR MATTED FLIES. As noted earlier, flies can become flattened or misshapen from improper storage. A dry fly in this condition may not sit properly on the water. If a streamer is stored wet with hair or feather wings in a bent position, the wings will remain distorted when the fly dries. They will usually relax and return to their original shape when the streamer is again saturated with water, but in the meantime the fly may twist, spin, or otherwise fish improperly.

Crumpled components on a fly can usually be restored by steaming them. Hold the fly by the hook bend in a pair of pliers or hemostats. A teakettle is the best source of steam since, unlike an open pan of boiling water, a kettle provides a jet of water vapor under low pressure. Hold the fly in the steam, moving or turning it slowly to let the vapor penetrate all the damaged areas until the bent fibers or crushed components relax to their normal position. You can help them along by letting the fly cool for a few seconds and gently preening the components back to shape. Depending on the size and condition of the fly, steaming can take as little as 15 seconds or as long as a couple of minutes. Let the fly dry thoroughly before returning it to your fly box.

VESTS

A fly-fishing vest requires the same kind of upkeep as any garment, and contrary to long-standing fishing tradition, this means washing it once in a while. Though it is a point of pride (or superstition) among many anglers never to clean a vest, the life of almost any article of clothing is extended if it is washed. Dirt that accumulates in the fabric weave is abrasive. I find cold water, a bleach-free detergent, and a gentle cycle to be the best. A vest is exposed to sunlight for long periods, and the UV rays will degrade almost any fabric. Overly aggressive washing can cause the fabric to tear. Then air-dry the vest.

If your vest uses hook-and-loop pocket closures, it's a good idea to sit down once a season or so and use a needle, toothpick, or dry toothbrush to clean the "hook" side of the fastener. This material is readily contaminated by threads and lint shed from the vest, fleece or wool fibers from clothing, bits of dried vegetation, and so on. The hooks eventually fill up with debris and lose their grip; the pocket flap won't close securely, and the contents can fall out.

When I clean the hook-and-loop material, I also empty out any zip-closing pockets, turn them inside out, and snip away any loose threads or fraying fabric edges than can find their way into the zipper track and cause it to jam.

RAIN JACKETS

Most rain jackets these days are made of waterproof/breathable material, and it's useful to think about their care and upkeep in the same way you think of maintaining waders.

CARE AND MAINTENANCE

The breathability of a wading jacket, like that of waders, is most efficient when the fabric is clean. If your jacket becomes excessively dirty or muddy during a day's fishing, simply rinse off the surface dirt. If you fish in salt water while wearing a jacket that has any metal hardware—zippers, snaps, D-rings—make sure to rinse off at least the metal components when you're done for the day.

Eventually dirt, grit, and salt residue will require a more thorough cleaning. Washing instructions vary with the jacket manufacturer and should be followed, but most can be machine washed (cold or warm water, no bleach or whiteners in the detergent) and line-dried. Make sure the jacket is completely dry before hanging it in a closet or storing it in a gear bag to prevent mildew.

Like waders, wading jackets are treated with a durable water repellent (DWR) finish on the exterior, and over time it will wear off. Waterproofness is not compromised, but the jacket fabric will cease to shed water, become waterlogged in the rain, feel heavy and uncomfortable, and take a long time to dry. The DWR can be restored in exactly the same way that you would re-treat waders, as explained on page 116.

REPAIR

Whether rips or holes in a wading jacket can be repaired depends primarily on whether or not the jacket has a lining. Many ultralightweight jackets are unlined, and they can be mended using the same techniques you'd use to patch wader leaks—with a dab of Aquaseal for small punctures or seam leaks, with iron-on or glued patches for larger rips and tears. Repairs to waterproof/breathable fabric are best performed on the interior surface since iron-on patches and glues often adhere better on the inside, though sometimes, patching the outside is the only way.

A jacket with a lining, however, presents a problem, since you can't get access to the inside surface of the jacket shell. Moreover, if you attempt a repair on the outside surface, you may end up gluing the jacket shell to the lining; the lining prevents you from placing tape or paper backing as a glue barrier behind the repair as you would patching waders. The only real solution is to cut through or detach part of the lining to expose the damaged area, and then resew the lining after the repair has been made. This is a fairly drastic measure, depending upon your facility with a needle and thread, but if an expensive or favorite jacket is torn, it may be worth the effort.

SUNGLASSES

Polarized sunglasses are without question one of the angler's most useful accessories and among the most delicate. Good ones are expensive and worth taking care of. Though accidental breakage is always a possibility, and many sunglasses meet their end this way, most of them become unusable from improper care of the lenses and frames.

PREVENTION

- Never lay your sunglasses, lenses-down, on a hard surface or keep them in a pocket with car keys, loose changes, or anything metallic.
- It's safest to wear sunglasses on a cord around your neck. They are reasonably protected, you won't lose them, and no one will sit on them.
- It's always best to store sunglasses in a hard case when you're not wearing them.
- Fashionable as it might be, wearing sunglasses on top of your head when you're not using them is a bad idea; it can eventually stretch the frames and make the glasses fit loosely.

- If the frames do need adjustment, you're better off taking them to an optician or optometrist, even if you must pay for the service. Improperly bending wire frames can stress solder joints and weaken them or torque the frame face to the point where the lenses no longer fit securely. Most plastic or nylon frames don't bend readily and are best adjusted by a professional. In a pinch, though, you can immerse the temples in a pan of hot water to soften the frame material slightly and then bend the temples into position. But never immerse the lenses, which can be damaged.

- By the same token, never expose sunglasses to excessive heat for a prolonged time—leaving them on the dashboard of a car, for instance. Synthetic frames can soften and deform, and the lenses, which are sandwiched around the polarizing filter, can delaminate.

- When putting on or removing sunglasses, use two hands, one on each temple. Grabbing one temple and pulling the glasses sideways off your face can stretch or bend the frames.

- Keep your glasses away from solvents; these can damage synthetic frames and lenses and lens coatings.

- If you drop your sunglasses in salt water, or if they get wet with spray, rinse them off in fresh water to prevent the hinges, screws, and other metal components from corroding.

CARE AND MAINTENANCE

The main concern in caring for sunglasses is keeping them clean. With the exception noted below, never dry-wipe your sunglasses or try to remove surface dirt on the lenses by rubbing them with your fingers or with a rough material such as wool, denim, or paper towels. And never try to remove a stubborn spot with your fingernail. Wiping a dirty, dry lens scrapes the abrasive particles of dirt, sand, and dried salt across the lens surface, and you can easily scratch softer lens materials. But even if the lenses are glass, which is relatively scratch resistant, you can damage the surface coatings used on many sunglasses to make the lenses water repellent or antireflective and end up with a spiderwebby haze.

Most manufacturers recommend cleaning sunglasses with a liquid lens cleaner or warm soapy water and drying them with a soft cloth. If you need to clean your glasses while fishing, at the very least swish them vigorously in the water to loosen and lift off any surface dirt, and dry them with a clean, soft fabric—a handkerchief or even a shirttail. Never use commercial home window cleaners that contain ammonia; these can strip some lens coatings.

Recently microfiber fabrics designed specifically for cleaning eyewear have become available. These are particularly handy since, under most circumstances, they can be used dry and are quite effective in removing dust, smudges, finger-prints, and oils. Heavy surface dirt, however, such as mud splashed on the lens, should still be rinsed off first.

Periodically check the hinge screws for tightness, and tighten them as needed. This is particularly prudent with frames that use spring-loaded temples; reinserting a screw while keeping the hinge holes aligned under spring tension can be tricky. Screws that repeatedly work loose can be secured using a very small amount of Loctite 242 Removable Threadlocker. I always pack a small eyeglass repair kit that contains a small screwdriver and extra screws; it's tiny, inexpensive, and almost weightless.

If you should happen to lose a hinge screw, don't use tape for the repair. Aside from making you look like the president of the junior high chess club, tape holds poorly in this application. Instead, line up the hinge holes, insert a length of 1X or 2X tippet materials, and knot it tightly. I actually wore sunglasses repaired like this for an entire season; it worked so well I kept forgetting they were broken.

CHECKLISTS

Aside from any repairs or maintenance that are necessary during the fishing season, I have over the years adopted an off-season routine for maintaining tackle to make sure that my gear is in good shape and ready for the upcoming year. I like to work on my tackle in stages; doing a little at a time makes it a pleasure rather than a chore. For what it's worth, here is my own regimen:

POSTSEASON WRAP-UP

I check over my tackle as soon as I can after my fishing for the year has ended, when tackle problems such as wader leaks, lost or broken items, worn boot soles, and so on are still fresh in my mind. Over the course of the winter, these kinds of matters are easily forgotten, not to be rediscovered until opening day. I keep a small notebook to log equipment problems, needed repair supplies, and items that need replacing. At the end of the season:

- Inspect and clean rods.
- Clean, inspect, and lubricate reels.
- Wash, inspect, and dress lines.
- Check over waders and boots.
- Inventory fly boxes for replacement patterns to tie or buy. If you buy flies, you may see the best prices of the year immediately after the season ends. But you may not always find what you need; fly inventories at shops and mail-order houses are typically at their lowest at this time of year.
- Store flies in plastic food-storage containers or the freezer.

MIDWINTER REPAIRS

The middle of winter is a good time for more involved repair projects such as rewrapping guides or resoling waders. Purchase the list of supplies you made after the season ended, and complete the needed repairs during the off-season months.

If you tie flies, now is the time to start.

PRESEASON PREP

A month or six weeks before the start of the new season, take stock of smaller matters.

- Inventory your vest for split shot, strike indicators, floatant, fly-line cleaner, leaders.
- Inspect the condition of zinger cords and nipper jaws.
- I usually replace nylon tippet material in sizes smaller than 3X and make sure I have spare spools of tippet in sizes I use often.
- Wash waders if they need it.
- Wash your vest if necessary, and clean off any hook-and-loop closures.
- Replace leaders on reels if necessary.
- Check your field kit and replace any items that were used up during the season.
- Purchase flies, leaders, or other items that are needed.

FIELD KIT

No serious angler I know travels anywhere—for a day or a month—without a field kit that has vital repair supplies. I pack them in a plastic food-storage container kept in a tackle bag that is always in my car or boat. I carry the items in italics in a zip-closing bag in the back of my vest.

- Small selection of extra tip-tops and snake guides (with the feet ground, ready for mounting)
- Spool of GSP or Kevlar thread
- Wader patches, Aquaseal, Cotol-240 Cure Accelerator
- Gel-type cyanoacrylate glue
- Single-edged razor blades
- Reel lubricants
- Selection of screws for repairing wader soles
- Finishing nail (for punching pilot holes for screws in boot soles)
- Screwdrivers or other tools sized to fit reels
- Duct tape, electrician's tape, and fiberglass packing tape (to reduce bulk, I usually wrap generous lengths of each type of tape on a length of wooden dowel)
- *Ferrule cement*
- *Extra bootlaces*

- *A couple of large safety pins (for fixing wader suspenders or vest rips)*
- *Multitool*
- *Eyeglass repair kit*
- *Line cleaner, dressing, and clean cloth*

Index